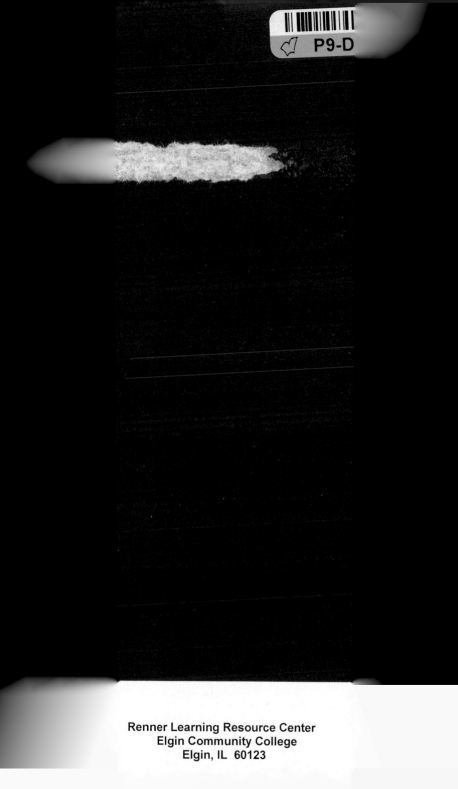

Renner Learning Resource Center
Elgin Community College
Elgin, IL 60123

War Law

War Law

*Understanding International Law
and Armed Conflict*

MICHAEL BYERS

GROVE PRESS
New York

RENNER LEARNING RESOURCE CENTER
ELGIN CO MMUNITY COL LEGE
ELGIN, ILLINOIS 601 23

341.6
B993w

Copyright © 2005 by Michael Byers

All rights reserved. No part of this book may be reproduced in any form or by any electronic or mechanical means, including information storage and retrieval systems, without permission in writing from the publisher, except by a reviewer, who may quote brief passages in a review. Any members of educational institutions wishing to photocopy part or all of the work for classroom use, or publishers who would like to obtain permission to include the work in an anthology, should send their inquiries to Grove/Atlantic, Inc., 841 Broadway, New York, NY 10003.

First published in Great Britain in 2005 by
Atlantic Books, an imprint of Grove Atlantic Ltd.

Printed in the United States of America

FIRST AMERICAN EDITION

Library of Congress Cataloging-in-Publication Data

Byers, Michael, 1966–
    War law : understanding international law and armed conflicts / Michael Byers.
      p. cm.
    Originally published: Great Britain : Atlantic Books, 2005.
    Includes bibliographical references and index.
    ISBN 0-8021-1809-7
    1. War (International law). 2. War—Causes. 3. Just war doctrine. I. Title.
KZ6385.B94 2006
341.6—dc22   2005045641

Grove Press
an imprint of Grove/Atlantic, Inc.
841 Broadway
New York, NY 10003

06 07 08 09 10   10 9 8 7 6 5 4 3 2 1

25.00

8-17-06

For Katharine

Contents

Foreword

The international law governing the use of military force has recently been the subject of intense public debate. Both the Kosovo War (1999) and the Iraq War (2003) sparked controversy as neither was expressly authorized by the United Nations Security Council. National leaders, including Bill Clinton, Tony Blair and George W. Bush, spoke openly about issues of international law. Pundits pontificated and millions of people marched in the streets, yet there was considerable confusion about the international rules of war.

This book aims to provide the interested non-lawyer with a readily comprehensible overview of the law governing the use of force in international affairs. It does so against the backdrop of recent political developments – including, most notably, the United States' rise to military predominance – in recognition of the intrinsic relationship between global politics and international law. Although this book is not intended for legal experts, references to further reading are provided for those who wish to delve more deeply into the issues.

Any book intended for a general readership will draw on diverse sources and experiences. Although more people deserve thanks than I could ever list here, I do wish to record my gratitude to certain individuals. Robert Byers, Michael Perry, Scott Silliman, Adriana Sinclair, Greta Smith and Nicholas Wheeler read and commented on the entire manuscript, while Kathy and Mike Edmunds provided the quiet English village environment in which most of the writing was done. The editors of the *London Review of Books* have long encouraged my efforts to explain the complexities of international law and politics to non-specialist audiences: portions of this book consolidate and expand upon some of the essays that I have written for them. And I am indebted to the many excellent students, from many countries, who have taken my courses on international law and the use of military force. Although we often disagreed, our lively discussions have greatly enriched my perspective on these controversial issues. In this sense, my students helped me write this book.

MB
Blewbury, Oxfordshire
20 December 2004

Introduction

During the lead-up to the Iraq War, on 6 February 2003, BBC *Newsnight* host Jeremy Paxman asked Prime Minister Tony Blair: 'Will you give an undertaking to this audience and indeed to the British people that before any military action you will seek another UN resolution specifically authorizing the use of force?'

Blair replied, 'Those are the only circumstances in which we would agree to use force, except for one caveat' – which, he explained, was if a veto was 'unreasonably' exercised by one of the five permanent members of the UN Security Council, thus blocking the adoption of a further resolution.

As the Prime Minister recognized, there are rules governing how countries behave. Most of the rules, concerning matters such as international postal services, air travel and trade, are obeyed almost all of the time; as a consequence, they are rarely noticed and generally uncontroversial. Other rules, such as those governing the use of military force, are highly politicized and the subject of frequent dispute. Blair, by introducing the concept of an 'unreasonable veto', was advancing a hotly contested – even bizarre – understanding of those rules. The United Nations Charter does not even hint at the concept of an unreasonable veto, nor have countries ever treated Security Council vetoes in this way. But Blair, torn between his personal commitment to join President George W. Bush's invasion of Iraq, and widespread domestic concern about the wisdom and legality of that action, was not above grasping at legal straws.

It should come as no surprise that the law on the use of force is politicized. Prussian military philosopher Carl von Clausewitz famously wrote that 'war is politics by other means'. And the stakes are particularly high in this particular sphere of politics, since war constitutes a direct challenge to the sovereignty, territorial integrity and political independence of nation-states. Nevertheless, governments pay considerable attention to the rules on the use of force – indeed, most governments, including the British and US governments, take these rules very seriously – since they directly protect and support *their* sovereignty, and not just the sovereignty of other countries. Tony Blair, even when advancing the novel concept of an 'unreasonable veto', neither rejected the existence of rules nor argued that none were applicable in the circumstances.

Historically speaking, legal rules on the use of military force are a relatively recent development. Prior to the adoption of the UN Charter in 1945, international law imposed few constraints on the recourse to arms. International law was conceived in strictly consensual terms during the nineteenth and early twentieth centuries: countries were only bound by those rules to which they had agreed, either through the conclusion of a treaty or through a consistent pattern of behaviour that, over time, gave rise to what is referred to as 'customary international law'. This consent-based conception of law is often referred to as 'positivism' to distinguish it from earlier conceptions of 'natural law' based on intuitions and interpretations of divine will. Today, consent remains central to international law. Although ethicists and scholars of canon law draw on natural law to distinguish between 'just' and 'unjust' wars, their thinking exists in a sphere that is separate from the rules regarded as binding by national governments.

Since governments had not agreed otherwise, military aggression was left largely unregulated until the UN Charter was adopted in 1945. Until this time, conquest gave good title to territory, as was demonstrated by the British acquisition of the Falkland Islands in 1833. The only rule concerning recourse to force was the right of self-defence, which, when properly exercised, enabled a country to use force without provoking all-out conflict. The introduction of legal limits on the use of force through the UN Charter was a transformative moment in international affairs, and it was entirely consensual. As US President

Harry Truman explained at the conference that founded the United Nations: 'We all have to recognize – no matter how great our strength – that we must deny ourselves the licence to do always as we please.'

Since 1945, governments that use force have almost always sought to justify their actions in legal terms, however tenuously. The United States advanced two legal arguments for the invasion of Iraq in March 2003: an extended right of pre-emptive self-defence and the enforcement of UN Security Council resolutions. Other countries, as they deliberated how to respond, assessed the merit of the legal claims. In some cases, their willingness to send troops, contribute financially, or at least provide access to military bases and airspace, was clearly influenced by their understanding of international law. In Britain, Attorney General Lord Goldsmith's public pronouncement on the legality of the war was a political prerequisite for Tony Blair's decision to take the country into the conflict. Similarly, the Turkish parliament's concerns about the illegality of the war resulted in the denial of Turkish territory for the deployment of US tanks into northern Iraq.

Illegal recourses to force will sometimes prompt countries to take forceful action in response. The invasion of Kuwait by Iraq in August 1990 was a clear violation of international law. Five months later, the Iraqi army was expelled from Kuwait by a coalition of approximately thirty countries expressly authorized to use force by the UN Security Council. In other instances, responses to illegal uses of force will be limited to economic sanctions or diplomatic measures against the law-breaking state. The refusal of many countries to aid the United States and Britain in and after the 2003 Iraq War can be explained, in part, by the profound difference of opinion on the legality of Operation Iraqi Freedom.

It is clear that the international rules on the use of force matter. But what exactly is international law, where does one find it, and how does one determine its rules?

There are two principal sources of international law, the first of which is customary international law, an informal, unwritten body of rules deriving from a combination of 'state practice' and *opinio juris*. State practice is what governments do and say; *opinio juris* is a belief, on the part of governments, that their conduct is obligated by international law.

Most rules of customary international law apply universally: they bind all countries and all countries contribute to their development and change. When a new rule of customary international law is being formed, every country has a choice: support the developing rule through its actions or statements, or actively and publicly oppose the rule. A new rule will not come into force until it receives widespread support.

Support for a customary rule does not need to be actively expressed. Acquiescence by a country in the face of a developing rule is sufficient. A country may thus be bound to a new rule as a result of doing nothing – a possibility that entails certain risks for unwary or understaffed governments. Most countries monitor the international legal system carefully to avoid becoming unwittingly bound by new customary rules.

Treaties are the second main source of international law. Treaties are contractual, written instruments entered into by two or more countries with the intent of creating binding rights and obligations and registered with a third party, nowadays usually the UN Secretary General. Treaties may be referred to by any number of different names, including 'charter', 'convention', 'covenant', 'exchange of notes' or 'protocol'.

Entering into – or concluding – a treaty typically requires a two-step process: 'signature' indicates a country's intention to assume obligations and 'ratification' is the point at which the obligations are formally undertaken. Non-lawyers often fail to distinguish between these two phases – which can lead to confusion when a country has signed, but not yet ratified, a treaty that would otherwise be relevant to a particular dispute. Complicating things further, the act of ratifying a treaty that has already entered into force between other countries is referred to as 'accession' rather than 'ratification'!

Countries ratify treaties in accordance with constitutional processes. In Britain, Canada and Australia, treaty ratification is an executive act by the government that does not require parliamentary approval. In the United States, a treaty cannot be ratified until the president receives the 'advice and consent' of two thirds of the members of the Senate. As a result, it is more difficult for the United States to ratify treaties, especially if the president and the majority of senators belong to different political parties. Republican Jesse Helms, a fierce opponent of international law, chaired the Senate Foreign Relations Committee during the last six years of the administration of President Bill Clinton, a Democrat. Politics in the process helps explain why some important treaties, such as the Comprehensive Test Ban Treaty (CTBT) on nuclear weapons, have not yet been ratified by the United States. Helms postponed bringing the CTBT to a vote until the height of the Monica Lewinsky scandal, when Clinton's influence was at its nadir.

Treaties are interpreted on the basis of agreed rules conveniently set out in a treaty of their own: the 1969 Vienna Convention on the Law of Treaties. The Vienna Convention is widely accepted – even by non-parties – as an accurate codification of the customary international law governing treaties. Accordingly, the rules set out in the Vienna Convention are binding on all countries. The most important rule concerning treaty interpretation is found in Article 31(1):

A treaty shall be interpreted in good faith in accordance with the ordinary meaning to be given to the terms of the treaty in their context and in the light of its object and purpose.

Giving words their *ordinary meaning* is the guiding principle of treaty interpretation. Treaties mean what they say. Yet in some instances the same word, or combination of words, can reasonably be understood to mean different things. In some instances, treaty interpretation requires a consideration of *context*, which generally involves reading the treaty as a whole. This process is frequently facilitated by 'preambles': non-binding paragraphs at the beginning of treaties that are meant to indicate their *object and purpose*. For example, when interpreting the UN Charter's provisions on the use of force, it is relevant that the preamble to the treaty expresses a determination to 'save succeeding generations from the scourge of war'.

A treaty provision prevails over any conflicting rule of customary international law. For this reason, countries sometimes conclude treaties in order to exempt aspects of their relations from otherwise applicable customary rules. For example, a government sending troops abroad will sometimes enter into a 'status of forces agreement' that exempts its soldiers from customary rules that would otherwise give the country to which they are being deployed jurisdiction over criminal and civil matters involving them.

Many rules of customary international law have been 'codified' into treaty provisions, while other customary practices have 'crystallized' into rules as a result of treaties replicating and thus reinforcing them. The UN Charter goes even further. In addition to codifying and crystallizing a number of customary rules, including a prohibition on the use of force and the right of self-defence, the Charter explicitly states that it prevails over all other treaties. Accordingly, countries cannot exempt themselves from the provisions of the UN Charter, which include the authority of the UN Security Council and the international rules governing recourse to military force.

This admittedly complex picture is rendered more complex by the existence of a few non-treaty rules of a 'peremptory' character. These special rules – called *jus cogens* rules – override conflicting rules, including conflicting treaty provisions. *Jus cogens* rules include the prohibitions on genocide, slavery and torture. The customary rule prohibiting the use of force, crystallized in the UN Charter, is also widely regarded as having achieved *jus cogens* status.

The UN Charter is thus the starting point for most issues

concerning international law and the use of force. Adopted in the immediate aftermath of the Second World War, the primary goal of the Charter was to provide clear rules on recourse to force, along with an institutional framework for enforcing the rules. The Charter has since been ratified by 192 countries.

The UN Charter's central provision is Article 2(4):

> All Members shall refrain in their international relations from the threat or use of force against the territorial integrity or political independence of any state, or in any other manner inconsistent with the Purposes of the United Nations.

The ordinary meaning of Article 2(4) is clear: the use of force across borders is not permitted. This meaning is supported by the Charter's context, object and purpose.

The UN Charter provides two exceptions to the prohibition set out in Article 2(4): authorization by the Security Council and self-defence. The Security Council, an executive body made up of fifteen countries, may authorize the use of force by adopting resolutions to that effect under a section of the Charter referred to as 'Chapter VII'. The central role of the Security Council in matters concerning recourse to force is the focus of the first three chapters of this book.

As for self-defence, Article 51 of the UN Charter stipulates:

> Nothing in the present Charter shall impair the inherent right of individual or collective self-defence if an armed attack occurs against a Member of the United Nations, until the Security Council has taken measures necessary to maintain international peace and security.

Article 51 is the focus of several debates. The first concerns whether one country may use force within the territory of another country against terrorists located there. In 1998 and 2001, the United States invoked self-defence to justify military action in

Afghanistan following terrorist attacks against US targets, first in Nairobi and Dar es Salaam, and then in New York City and Washington, DC. Similarly, Israel claims self-defence when engaging in the 'targeted killing' of Palestinian leaders in the Gaza Strip and West Bank. The Bush Administration has accepted the Israeli claim, while European governments regard the same acts as 'extra-judicial killings', which are illegal under international law.

Another debate over self-defence concerns whether, and to what degree, the exception includes a right of pre-emptive or anticipatory military action. Prior to 1945, countries were widely considered to have a right of pre-emption if there was a 'necessity of self-defence, instant, overwhelming, leaving no choice of means, and no moment of deliberation'. The adoption of Article 51 of the UN Charter, permitting self-defence only 'if an armed attack occurs', would then seem to have rendered pre-emptive action illegal (that is, unless it has been authorized by the UN Security Council).

Since 2002, the United States has sought to develop a right of pre-emptive self-defence that extends to more distant and uncertain challenges, most notably those arising out of the combined threat of weapons of mass destruction and global terrorism. Although the so-called 'Bush Doctrine' remains highly controversial, it has been endorsed by several other countries, notably Israel and Russia. The right of self-defence is the focus of the fourth, fifth and sixth chapters of this book.

Two further, unwritten exceptions to the prohibition on the use of force may have developed in recent decades. The first is a right to intervene militarily to promote or restore democracy. Proponents of this exception point to the US-led interventions in Grenada in 1983 and Panama in 1989 as precedents. They also claim that advancements in international human rights have displaced sovereignty away from governments and into the hands of ordinary people; consequently, governments that deny the popular will are no longer sovereign and cannot benefit from the prohibition on the use of force.

The second possible additional exception involves a right to intervene on humanitarian grounds in the event of heinous abuses such as genocide, mass expulsion or systematic rape. Proponents of this right of unilateral humanitarian intervention – 'unilateral' because the interventions are not authorized by the UN Security Council – point to the creation of 'no-fly' zones in Iraq in 1991 and the 1999 Kosovo War as precedents. And like the proponents of a right of pro-democratic intervention, they argue that developments in international human rights favour the use of force against abusive governments. The seventh, eighth and ninth chapters of this book consider pro-democratic intervention, unilateral humanitarian intervention, and the related concept of a 'responsibility to protect'.

In addition to rules governing recourse to force, there are rules concerning how soldiers behave once armed conflict has begun. The four Geneva Conventions of 1949 are treaties that set out a body of law referred to as the 'laws of war', 'law of armed conflict' or 'international humanitarian law'. The latter term (also known as *jus in bello*) is preferred because it indicates that the rules protect individuals rather than nation-states.

Any armed conflict involves two broad categories of individuals: combatants and non-combatants (who are also referred to as civilians). International humanitarian law protects both categories of persons, though non-combatants are shielded more than those who take up arms. The most important protection for non-combatants is a requirement that the risk to them be factored into all military decisions. Purely civilian targets cannot be selected, while the targeting of 'dual-use facilities' such as electrical grids and sewage treatment plants must be assessed very carefully on a case-by-case basis. During the Kosovo War, the destruction of water filtration plants and a television station by the North Atlantic Treaty Organization (NATO) caused considerable controversy, though the prosecutor for the International Criminal Tribunal for the former Yugoslavia did not subsequently indict any NATO personnel.

Combatants are protected from weapons and means of warfare that cause unnecessary suffering, including chemical and biological weapons and bullets designed to explode on impact. Soldiers are entitled to surrender and receive a range of protections as prisoners of war (POWs). POWs may not be punished for having taken up arms and are entitled to be treated with dignity; they must also be released once the hostilities have come to an end. Yet the mistreatment of POWs is far too common. During the 2003 Iraq War, some captured US troops were mistreated by their Iraqi captors. After the invasion, many Iraqis in US custody were also abused.

Individuals who break the rules may be tried for war crimes before national courts or international tribunals. The Nuremberg and Tokyo Tribunals, established following the Second World War, have served as models for international tribunals for the former Yugoslavia and Rwanda. In 1998, negotiators from 120 countries established a permanent International Criminal Court (ICC). The ICC has been the subject of considerable controversy, largely because the United States has actively sought to undermine it. At the same time, the trials of Slobodan Milošević before the Yugoslav tribunal in The Hague and of Saddam Hussein before an Iraqi court in Baghdad have demonstrated the relative strengths of international and national proceedings. International humanitarian law and war crimes tribunals are dealt with in the tenth, eleventh and twelfth chapters of this book.

Much of this book refers to actions by the United States, which, in relative terms, is militarily more powerful than any political entity since the Roman Empire. Thanks to its massive defence spending – as much as the next twenty countries combined – the United States is also the only country that regularly makes major advances in military technology. It backs up its hardware and budget with an aggressive policy of forward staging: US troops are now based in more than 140 countries.

The United States has long demonstrated a willingness to use its military power in legally questionable circumstances, most recently in Kosovo and Iraq. The United States also consciously seeks to modify international law in accordance with its interests, for instance, by pushing for a right of self-defence against terrorism, and for the Bush Doctrine of pre-emptive self-defence. Over time, the combination of predominant military power and the deliberate pursuit of normative change will test, stretch and sometimes alter the limits of international law. Yet the existence of a militarily dominant, legally entrepreneurial state does not necessarily spell the end of the global rules on the use of force. International law is made and changed by all of the nearly 200 countries in this world and is indirectly influenced by an even larger number of non-governmental actors, such as international organizations and human rights groups.

The United States itself needs international law, if sometimes only to persuade other countries of the legitimacy of its actions and to secure their participation and support. As the high costs of the occupation of Iraq demonstrate, America pays a price for ignoring world opinion. Even in the highly politicized sphere of military action, and even for the single superpower, the question is not whether international law exists, but how and when it matters. The epilogue to this book considers the unique position of the United States – and of committed allies such as Tony Blair – as they shape, break and attempt to remake the international rules on the use of military force.

Part One

United Nations Action

Security Council Authorization

In 1945, representatives from fifty countries gathered in San Francisco to create a new international organization: the United Nations. The negotiations took place in the aftermath of the Second World War with its tens of millions of casualties, including the millions of civilians slaughtered during the Holocaust and the hundreds of thousands who were to die as a result of the atomic bombings of Hiroshima and Nagasaki. The diplomats sought an institution and set of rules that would, in their words, 'save succeeding generations from the scourge of war'. The treaty they negotiated – the Charter of the United Nations – focused on preserving the peace and empowering multilateral responses to threats or breaches of the peace. One hundred and ninety-two countries have since ratified the UN Charter and are thereby 'member states' of the United Nations with all the rights and obligations that entails.

Again, the central obligation of membership is set out in Article 2(4) of the UN Charter:

All Members shall refrain in their international relations from the threat or use of force against the territorial integrity or political independence of any state, or in any other manner inconsistent with the Purposes of the United Nations.

Interpreted according to the 1969 Vienna Convention on the Law of Treaties, the ordinary meaning of Article 2(4) is clear: the use of force across borders is categorically prohibited. This interpretation is supported by the Charter's context, object and purpose. The preamble to the UN Charter states that it is designed to 'ensure by the acceptance of principles and the institution of methods, that armed force shall not be used, save in the common interest'. The Charter sets out only two exceptions to the prohibition on the use of force. The first exception empowers the UN Security Council, a specialized decision-making body made up of representatives from fifteen member states of the United Nations, to authorize the use of force 'to maintain or restore international peace and security'.

Of the fifteen countries on the Security Council, five – Britain, China, France, the United States and the Soviet Union (now Russia) – are designated as 'permanent members'. Each permanent member has the power to veto any proposed resolution. Sometimes the mere threat of a veto is enough to prevent a resolution from being put to a vote. In the absence of a veto, nine votes are required for a resolution to pass. This requirement means that the support of at least four non-permanent members is needed for any resolution to be adopted, and more than four in the event that one or more permanent members choose to abstain from voting. In early 2003, the British government's decision not to put its so-called 'second resolution' on Iraq to a vote was conditioned as much by opposition from non-permanent members as it was by the threat of a French or Russian veto.

Under Chapter VII of the UN Charter, the Security Council has a broad authority to 'determine the existence of any threat to the peace, breach of the peace, or act of aggression'. The Council has an equally broad authority to decide which measures shall be taken to 'maintain or restore international peace and security'. Such measures can include imposing economic sanctions and, even more significantly, authorizing the use of military force against disobedient countries.

During the Cold War, the UN Security Council's power to authorize the use of force went largely unexercised, apart from an ambiguous, possible authorization in Korea and a clear but very constrained authorization to the United Kingdom with regard to Southern Rhodesia.

*

North Korea's invasion of South Korea in 1950 prompted the newly created Security Council to 'recommend' that UN member states 'furnish such assistance to South Korea as may be necessary to repel the armed attack and to restore international peace and security in the area'. The resolution was highly controversial. First, the Soviet Union boycotted the Council meeting at which the resolution was passed. According to an ordinary meaning interpretation of Article 27(3) of the UN Charter, which stipulates that substantive resolutions must receive the 'concurring votes' of all the permanent members, the Soviet Union's absence should have prevented adoption of the resolution. Nevertheless, most governments treated the resolution as valid. Second, since the resolution was recommending – rather than expressly authorizing – the use of force, it was questionable whether the Security Council was actually using its Chapter VII powers.

The Korean War had an important consequence for the international law on the use of force. Today, it is widely accepted that absences or abstentions by one or more permanent members of the Security Council are not fatal to resolutions under vote. If a permanent member wishes to block a resolution, it must actually cast a negative vote. Permanent members are now careful to attend all Security Council meetings lest their absence facilitate the lawmaking efforts of states whose policies they oppose.

In 1964, Ian Smith, the leader of the Rhodesian Front, became prime minister of the British colony of Southern Rhodesia. After failing to persuade London to set the colony free, Smith and his government made a 'unilateral declaration of independence' – under white minority rule – on 11 November 1965.

The UN General Assembly, a body made up of all UN member states, had adopted its first resolution on Rhodesia in 1961. The resolution deplored 'the denial of equal political rights and liberties to the vast majority of the people of Southern Rhodesia'. However, the General Assembly can only recommend – and not authorize – economic sanctions or military action. Accordingly, the Assembly responded to the 1965 Rhodesian declaration of independence by condemning it as a 'rebellion' by 'unlawful authorities' and a 'racialist minority' and recommending that the Security Council consider the situation 'as a matter of urgency'.

The Security Council condemned 'the usurpation of power by a racist settler minority', stating that the declaration of independence had 'no legal validity'. The Council also called upon countries to break all economic ties with Rhodesia, but neither imposed legally binding sanctions nor authorized the use of force.

Five months later, the Security Council learned that substantial quantities of oil were about to reach landlocked Rhodesia from tankers offloading oil into a pipeline that ran from the Mozambique port of Beira. The Council responded with Resolution 221, which deemed the situation a 'threat to the peace'. Most importantly, the resolution called upon the United Kingdom 'to prevent, by the use of force if necessary, the arrival of vessels reasonably believed to be carrying oil destined for Southern Rhodesia'.

Although the language of Resolution 221 did not expressly refer to the Security Council's powers under Chapter VII, the resolution was probably the first occasion on which that part of the UN Charter was used. That the resolution was adopted at all is remarkable, given the intense Cold War rivalry between the two veto-holding superpowers. The specific nature of the Rhodesian situation – a white racist minority rebellion in a part of the world where the Soviet Union and United States were competing for influence over newly independent black governments – helps explain its adoption, as do the narrowly defined limits of the apparent authorization given to the UK.

Eight months later, in December 1966, the Security Council imposed the first mandatory economic sanctions in UN history. In Resolution 232, the Council again determined that the situation in Rhodesia constituted a threat to international peace and security. Using the words 'all State Members of the United Nations shall prevent' to avoid any ambiguity, the resolution prohibited the import of any of Rhodesia's principal products, as well as the export of arms, oil or oil products to the country. The mandatory embargo was later broadened to sever air links, ban the acceptance of Rhodesian passports, withdraw all consular and trade representatives from the country and break off diplomatic relations and ground transportation links.

It took almost a decade, but these external pressures eventually led to all-party talks at Lancaster House in London in 1979. The talks produced a peace agreement and a new constitution for the country that guaranteed minority rights. In 1980, Robert Mugabe and his Zanu Party won British-supervised elections. Mugabe was named prime minister and, on 18 April 1980, the colony of Southern Rhodesia became the independent country of Zimbabwe. Although the Security Council's authorization of the use of force played only a minimal role in the international effort that ultimately led to a sovereign Zimbabwe, Resolution 221 is a milestone in the ongoing development of international rules on the use of force, and of Chapter VII of the UN Charter in particular.

The Security Council's period of general inactivity, coinciding with the Cold War, ceased after the Iraqi army invaded and seized the small neighbouring country of Kuwait on 2 August 1990. The invasion was a blatant violation of the UN Charter and its prohibition in Article 2(4) on the use of force against the 'territorial integrity and political independence' of any UN member state. The Security Council responded the very next day, adopting Resolution 660. Acting expressly under Chapter VII, the Council condemned the invasion and demanded Iraq's immediate withdrawal from Kuwait. A few days later, the Council imposed stringent mandatory economic sanctions on Iraq.

Four months of intense diplomatic activity followed as world leaders sought to persuade Iraqi president Saddam Hussein to comply with international law and the orders of the Security Council. When Saddam refused, the Security Council increased its pressure. On 29 November 1990, the Council adopted Resolution

678 in which it 'decided to allow Iraq one final opportunity' to remove its forces from Kuwait, and set a deadline of 15 January 1991. This was not an empty gesture. Resolution 678, which like Resolution 660 was expressly adopted under Chapter VII, went on to authorize countries co-operating with the government of Kuwait to 'use all necessary means' to remove the Iraqi forces and 'restore international peace and security in the area' – in the event that Iraq failed to withdraw its troops. The phrase 'use all necessary means' was clearly intended to authorize the use of military force.

By the time the deadline arrived, the US-led coalition had deployed nearly 700,000 troops to the region; they subsequently needed little time to remove Saddam's forces from Kuwait. Operation Desert Storm was a resounding success, not only militarily, but also for the authority of the Security Council and the broader UN. President George H. W. Bush spoke proudly of the 'new world order' that was reflected in this exercise in global multilateralism. Unfortunately, Bush's new order was remarkably fragile, as events in the Balkans soon demonstrated.

War consumed Bosnia-Herzegovina from April 1992 to November 1995, following the collapse of the Federal Republic of Yugoslavia and the eruption of ethnic tensions that since the Second World War had been largely suppressed by totalitarian rule. A defining feature of the conflict was the prevalence of ethnically motivated killings, rapes and expulsions, primarily involving Muslim victims. During the first five months of the conflict, more than 700,000 people were driven from an area covering 70 per cent of Bosnia-Herzegovina. The atrocities committed fell within the scope of the 1948 Convention on the Prevention and Punishment of the Crime of Genocide (the Genocide Convention), Article 2 of which states:

> In the present Convention, genocide means any of the following acts committed with intent to destroy, in whole or in part, a national, ethnical, racial or religious group, as such:

(a) Killing members of the group;
(b) Causing serious bodily or mental harm to members of the group;
(c) Deliberately inflicting on the group conditions of life calculated to bring about its physical destruction in whole or in part;
(d) Imposing measures intended to prevent births within the group;
(e) Forcibly transferring children of the group to another group.

During the Bosnian War, most journalists and state officials too readily adopted the Serbian euphemism 'ethnic cleansing' to describe the horrors that were taking place. The use of this label enabled Western governments to avoid the groundswell of public opinion that would likely have arisen had they invoked the more accurate, morally resonant word 'genocide'. It may even have been an attempt by those same governments to shirk their responsibility 'to prevent and to punish' genocide under Article 1 of the Genocide Convention. However, evasive terminology did not prevent public evocations of the Holocaust in describing the situation in Bosnia. Some 250,000 people were killed, thousands more were tortured and starved in concentration camps, millions lost their homes and countless women were raped and forcibly impregnated – and all this in a rapidly unifying, post-Cold War Europe that had as one of its central missions the promotion of human rights.

Shortly after the war began, the UN Security Council passed Resolution 713. Adopted expressly under Chapter VII of the UN Charter, the resolution imposed an arms embargo on all of the former Yugoslavia. The embargo arguably did more harm than good because it preserved a military imbalance between the Serbian forces, who had acquired most of the heavy weapons of the previous Yugoslav army, and the less well-armed Bosnian Muslims. The United States later sought to rescind the resolution and lift the embargo, but was unable to do so because of opposition by Russia, which was concerned about US influence in the region and identified religiously with the Eastern Orthodox Serbs. The arms embargo against the former Yugoslavia remained in force until the Dayton Accords brought an end to the conflict in November 1995, though weapons were smuggled into the country, some with the assistance of the United States.

In 1992, the UN Security Council, acting under Chapter VII, established the United Nations Protection Force (UNPROFOR) to provide peacekeeping – the non-violent monitoring of ceasefires, including by providing a neutral presence in buffer zones – in the former Yugoslavia. In 1993, the Security Council extended the force's mandate to include the creation and protection of 'safe havens' in Bosnia. The same year, again acting under Chapter VII, the Council took the novel step of creating an international tribunal to prosecute individuals who had allegedly committed atrocities and to deter further violations of international law. The International Criminal Tribunal for the former Yugoslavia (ICTY), located in The Hague, is a subsidiary organ of the UN Security Council. The ICTY has jurisdiction to investigate and prosecute war crimes and crimes against humanity committed in the former Yugoslavia since 1991. This jurisdiction continued through the 1999 Kosovo War and remains in place today. Moreover, since the ICTY was created by a Chapter VII resolution and not by a treaty, the tribunal's jurisdiction took effect immediately – without the need for the consent of individual countries. Slobodan Milošević, the former President of Yugoslavia, was thus unable to avoid the tribunal, and has been on trial in The Hague since 2001. In 1994, the UN Security Council followed the model of the ICTY in creating the International Criminal Tribunal for Rwanda, though the jurisdiction of this tribunal is limited to events occurring during 1994, the year the genocide took place. Both tribunals served as influential models for the International Criminal Court, a permanent institution with much broader jurisdiction, the treaty for which was adopted in 1998 and entered into force in 2002. They have also obtained a number of convictions, generated valuable precedents on questions of international criminal law, and generally helped advance international justice elsewhere.

In 1993, NATO, embarrassed by massacres in the UN 'safe havens' in the former Yugoslavia, and Europe's failure to stop them, bombed Serbian weapons and supply lines in Bosnia. The bombing was conducted under a complex mandate, provided through UN Security Council Resolution 836 of 4 June 1993, which required close cooperation on targeting decisions between NATO and then UN Secretary General Boutros Boutros-Ghali. The agreement proved unwieldy and ineffective. In July 1995, more than 7,000 Muslim men and boys were slaughtered in the 'safe haven' of Srebrenica as 400 Dutch peacekeepers stood by, their pleas for NATO air support unanswered. In 2001, the ICTY confirmed that the massacre was an act of genocide when it convicted Radislav Krstic, the Yugoslav general in charge, and sentenced him to forty-six years in prison.

International efforts to restore peace to the former Yugoslavia were, on the whole, embarrassingly ineffective, not due to any lack of international law but because of a near absence of international political will. The lack of political will continues today: in December 2004, Carla del Ponte, the ICTY prosecutor, publicly chided NATO governments for having done little over the course of a decade to bring two of the principal alleged perpetrators of the atrocities in Bosnia-Herzegovina, Radovan Karadzic and Ratko Mladic, to justice. That the two indicted men remain at liberty in the eastern mountains of Bosnia is chilling evidence of the transitory and opportunistic character of most international efforts to prevent or punish international crimes.

That said, the four situations discussed in this chapter – Korea (1950), Southern Rhodesia (1966), Iraq (1990–91) and Bosnia-Herzegovina (1992–5) – saw the UN Security Council exercise its Chapter VII powers to authorize force in new and quite different ways. With the exception of Iraq, however, the consistent theme of this period was one of hesitation, as the politics of the Council, an inherently political body, prevented it from acting decisively and expansively to maintain and restore the peace. This disappointing picture began to change in the 1990s, as the next chapter explains.

Expanding Reach of the Security Council

Chapter VII of the UN Charter empowers the Security Council to authorize the use of force in response to threats and breaches of international peace. Yet the definition of this role – and therefore the scope of Security Council action – has expanded in recent years.

The Security Council's actions in Korea and Iraq were directed at cross-border military conflicts of the kind originally associated with Chapter VII. The Council's involvement in the domestic affairs of Southern Rhodesia departed from that model but was not considered a precedent because of the unusual mix of legalized racism, stymied self-determination of the black population, and superpower rivalry involved in the situation. The Council's actions in Bosnia-Herzegovina, driven by a combination of traditional inter-state security concerns and not-so-traditional worries about human rights atrocities, were of greater legal significance. The use of Chapter VII to create 'safe havens' and an international criminal tribunal was part of a broader move by the Council to include internal humanitarian crises within the concept of 'threats to international peace and security'.

During the 1990s, the UN Security Council determined that a number of domestic humanitarian and human rights crises constituted 'threats to international peace and security', justifying the use of its Chapter VII powers to impose mandatory sanctions or authorize the use of military force. In doing so, the Security Council went beyond the traditional conception of threats, though not in a manner that violated the UN Charter – since the Charter grants the Council broad discretion to determine the

RENNER LEARNING RESOURCE CENTER
ELGIN COMMUNITY COLLEGE
ELGIN, ILLINOIS 601 23

scope of its own legal competence. In several instances, notably Haiti in 1994 and East Timor in 1999, Chapter VII was more important in providing legitimacy than legality, as the actions there occurred at the invitation of the country that was subject to the intervention. In other instances, such as Somalia, Rwanda, and more recently Darfur, Sudan, there has been insufficient political will either to intervene promptly, or to persevere when the going gets tough.

In January 1992, the UN Security Council determined that the combination of widespread civil strife and devastating famine in Somalia constituted a threat to international peace and security. Although the Security Council spoke of the consequences of the strife and famine for 'stability and peace in the region', the determination extended the Council's reach under international law. In the 'new world order' that still seemed possible following the fall of the Berlin Wall and the 1991 Iraq War, the Security Council was asserting a scope of competence that stretched security into humanitarian and human rights concerns. Having determined the existence of a threat, the Council imposed a mandatory arms embargo on Somalia, but did not, at this early stage, authorize military action.

Three months later, with the chaos growing worse and hundreds of thousands of people starving, the Council inched towards the deployment of troops, requesting that the UN Secretary General, Boutros Boutros-Ghali, deploy fifty UN observers to monitor the situation. This operation, referred to as the United Nations Operations in Somalia (UNSOM), was expanded in August of 1992. Yet it remained a lightly armed peacekeeping operation, despite the fact that the Somali government had collapsed and warlords ran rampant. In recognition of this, the Security Council in December 1992 adopted a further resolution that led to two UN-authorized deployments: an additional 3,500 soldiers for the UNSOM force, and a second, US-led multinational force with a broad mandate to 'use all necessary means to establish as soon as possible a secure environment for humanitarian relief operations'. Unlike UNSOM, the US-led force was empowered to engage in 'peacemaking' rather than 'peacekeeping'; in other words, it had wide discretion to use military force.

In March 1993, the UN Security Council changed the name of the first deployment from UNSOM to UNSOM II, increased its size, and extended its mandate to include the disarmament of local militia groups and repatriation of refugees. The UN commander of the operation was also directed 'to assume responsibility for the consolidation, expansion and maintenance of a secure environment throughout Somalia'. This task was too much for a force lacking heavy weapons and air support. On 5 June 1993, twenty-three Pakistani peacekeepers were ambushed and killed by members of a Somali militia. The Security Council responded to the attack by increasing the size of UNSOM II to 28,000 soldiers, affirming its mandate to 'arrest and detain' the individuals responsible for the killings, and urging UN member states – and the parallel US-led operation by implication – to provide UNSOM II with military support and transportation.

On 3 October 1993, eighteen US Army Rangers were killed while attempting to apprehend Somali militia leaders. Television footage of a Ranger's body being dragged through the streets of Mogadishu prompted a public outcry in the United States that soon led to the withdrawal of all US forces from Somalia and the subsequent collapse of both the US- and UN-led operations. One American officer commented during the ignominious retreat that US soldiers would again operate under foreign command 'as soon as it snows in Mogadishu'. Ironically, the US troops had remained under US command and control at all times. The United Nations had simply provided a legal basis for their presence in Somalia and legitimized their actions.

Although the Somalia experience substantially diminished political will in the United States and elsewhere to engage in military interventions for purely humanitarian purposes, it constituted an important precedent for the international rules on the use of force. For the first time, the UN Security Council had deemed a human rights crisis a threat to the peace and used its Chapter VII powers to authorize military intervention for the sole purpose of preventing further suffering.

Rwanda suffered for the sins of the Somali warlords. 'Genocide', defined in the 1948 Genocide Convention as the 'intent to destroy, in whole or in part, a national, ethnical, racial or religious group', is more than a crime against humanity prohibited by a *jus cogens* rule. The term has acquired enormous moral approbation, to the point that, during a 1994 Security Council meeting on Rwanda, the British ambassador cautioned against designating the ethnically motivated massacre of 800,000 Tutsis as genocide because the Council might then be compelled to act. Not until Mary Robinson broke the taboo, shortly after her appointment as UN High Commissioner for Human Rights in 1997, did the term achieved common usage in contemporary international affairs. This paradigm shift facilitated the subsequent creation of the International Criminal Court, and influenced NATO's decision to intervene in Kosovo.

As the mass slaughter of Tutsi men, women and children by Hutus began, General Roméo Dallaire, the Canadian commander of the small UN operation in Kigali, pleaded for 5,000 additional troops. Bizarrely, the UN Security Council responded by reducing Dallaire's force from 2,500 to 270 peacekeepers. It was not until the bloodbath was nearly over that France announced it would send forces into the country whose Hutu militia it had armed and trained. Seized with misgivings, but knowing that no other country was prepared to act, and that an intervention without UN authorization could create an awkward precedent, the Security Council ultimately adopted a Chapter VII resolution that authorized *Opération Turquoise*. The resolution, and the French intervention that followed, came too late to do more than protect the Hutu *génocidaires* from Tutsi retribution. But the adoption of the resolution, scandalously inadequate though it was, constituted another instance of the Council authorizing military action to address a purely internal crisis.

The only other action taken by the UN Security Council was to create the International Criminal Tribunal for Rwanda (ICTR), which has since convicted more than twenty high-level perpetrators and further developed international criminal law – for example, by expanding the scope of the crime of genocide to include the incitement of genocide. In September 1998, Jean Kambanda, the former prime minister of Rwanda, was convicted of genocide by the ICTR for having encouraged a radio station to promote the extermination of Tutsis in 1994. That same month, the Rwandan tribunal gave another boost to international criminal law by convicting a former mayor, Jean-Paul Akayesu, of genocide for inciting others to systematically rape Tutsi women.

Like Rwanda, the Caribbean country of Haiti has a turbulent history. Achieving independence in 1804 after a slave rebellion against French colonialism, Haiti became the first post-colonial country in the Western hemisphere to be governed by non-whites. The United States occupied the country between 1915 and 1934, concerned that civil unrest was threatening its foreign investments. But Haiti suffered its worst period from 1956 to 1986 when it was governed by two brutal dictators, first François 'Papa Doc' Duvalier, and then his son Jean-Claude 'Baby Doc'. Two military coups in quick succession subsequently led to the creation of a civilian government under military control, though it took four years and repeated urgings from the Organization of American States (OAS) before democratic elections were held.

International monitors certified the 1990 election as free and fair and Jean-Bertrand Aristide, a Roman Catholic priest of humble origins, was elected president. But a *coup d'état* soon led to the resumption of military rule; Aristide was sent into exile in the United States in September 1991.

The OAS promptly condemned the coup and recommended economic and diplomatic sanctions. The UN General Assembly likewise quickly criticized the 'illegal replacement of the constitutional President of Haiti' and affirmed the unacceptability of 'any entity resulting from that illegal situation'. However, the UN Security Council failed to respond with comparable speed, reportedly because China, a veto-holding permanent member, had reservations about the Council's increasing involvement in areas traditionally considered within the domestic jurisdiction of states.

The Haitian military, undeterred by the harsh words of toothless international bodies, refused to reinstate the Aristide government. The refusal, along with reports of the widespread persecution of Aristide's supporters, eventually prompted the Security Council to exercise its Chapter VII powers. In June 1993, the Council imposed a mandatory economic embargo on Haiti. The resolution reflected China's concerns, listing specific factors that had led the Council to determine 'that, in these unique and exceptional circumstances, the continuation of this situation threatens international peace and security in the region'. The factors included 'the incidence of humanitarian crises, including mass displacements of population', and the 'climate of fear of persecution and economic dislocation which could increase the number of Haitians seeking refuge in neighbouring Member States'.

The reference to Haitian refugees was prompted by thousands of people who were escaping the country on rickety boats and rafts, many of them setting out for Florida. These refugees were of concern to the United States, but they were also important to China because they brought an international dimension to the situation that could justify Security Council action on more traditional, state-to-state security grounds. In practical terms, the international element of the crisis was barely significant. The number of refugees was relatively small and the US Coast Guard was already reducing that number to pre-coup levels through an aggressive interdiction and return programme. Chinese protestations aside, the Security Council had again departed from the traditional conception of what constituted a threat to 'international peace and security'.

The mandatory economic embargo had almost immediate effect, prompting the Haitian *junta* to accept terms – set out in the 'Governors Island Agreement' – whereby Aristide would be returned to power and the sanctions lifted. However, the agreement quickly collapsed when violence against Aristide supporters resumed one month later. The Security Council responded by reimposing sanctions and authorizing a naval blockade.

On 29 July 1994, nearly three years after the coup, Aristide himself requested 'prompt and decisive action' by the United Nations. Two days later, the Security Council again invoked Chapter VII. Resolution 940 'authorized Member States to form a multilateral force' and 'use all necessary means' to remove the *junta*, restore the legitimate government and 'establish and maintain a secure and stable environment' in Haiti.

Within six weeks, the United States had formed an 'international force' composed primarily of its own soldiers. Only a last-minute agreement secured by former President Jimmy Carter prevented a forceful invasion. By the end of September 1994, over 17,000 US troops were peacefully deployed in Haiti and Aristide had returned to Port-au-Prince. International reaction to the events was generally positive – as indeed it should have been. Only a handful of countries expressed reservations about the behaviour of the Security Council and the United States.

The Security Council's actions on Haiti confirm that the Council considers itself legally competent to impose mandatory sanctions and authorize military force in response to internal humanitarian crises that pose little, if any, threat to other countries. This self-assignment of competence is difficult to challenge because nothing in the UN Charter limits the Council's capacity to determine if and when a situation constitutes a threat to international peace and security. As the UN Secretary General's High Level Panel on Threats, Challenges and Change reported in December 2004, 'the Council and the wider international community have come to accept that, under Chapter VII... it can always authorize military action to redress catastrophic internal wrongs if it is prepared to declare that the situation is a "threat to international peace and security", not especially difficult when breaches of international law are involved.'

Some academics point to the Security Council actions in Haiti as an example of growing recognition of a right to 'pro-democratic intervention' in international law, as is discussed in Chapter 7 of this book. Yet the invocation of Chapter VII of the UN Charter deprived the incident of any value as a precedent for a right to unilateral intervention. A careful reading of Resolution 940 also reveals that the disruption of democracy was referred to as only one of several factors – together with the 'systematic violations of civil liberties' and 'desperate plight' of the refugees – that contributed to the finding of a threat to international peace and security. Moreover, the resolution was the direct result of the Aristide government-in-exile's request for UN action. Although the Security Council, acting under Chapter VII, is legally competent to authorize interventions without an invitation from a legitimate government, such an invitation – even from a government in exile – is widely acknowledged as a sufficient basis for the deployment of military assistance. And the legitimacy of governments, and thus the legal justification of intervention by invitation, is not dependent on the democratic character of the inviting state.

Nor does the democratic character of a government necessarily provide protection against unwanted intervention, as Jean-Bertrand Aristide himself discovered in 2004. Aristide's peaceful return to Haiti ten years earlier had brought some hope to that beleaguered country. In 1995, his supporters won parliamentary elections; in 1996, he resigned as president, abiding by a constitutional provision prohibiting two consecutive terms in office. Aristide's elected successor, René Preval, proved less than effective: at one point he desperately declared that the Haitian parliament's term had expired, and began ruling by decree. Preval stood down at the end of his term in 2001, at which point Aristide was re-elected president.

Meanwhile, Haiti – already the poorest country in the Western hemisphere – was subjected to stringent US sanctions and a sharp decline in foreign aid that together brought it to the edge of economic collapse and civil chaos. An attempted *coup d'état* in 2001 was followed in 2004 by a violent uprising of disgruntled ex-soldiers and gang members headed by Butteur Metayer, the former leader of a gang known as the 'Cannibal Army'. Dozens of people were killed, and, on the night of 28–29 February 2004, Aristide was flown to the Central African Republic on a plane chartered by the US military. Although the United States claimed he had left the country voluntarily, Aristide insisted that he had been forced out at gunpoint, an assertion given greater credibility when the Caribbean Community (CARICOM) refused to recognize the government of the new president. Aristide later travelled to Jamaica before moving on to South Africa, where the government of President Thabo Mbeki accorded him sanctuary.

The day after Aristide's flight from Haiti, the UN Security Council unanimously adopted Resolution 1529, which authorized a multilateral force to restore law and order to the country. Within days, soldiers from the United States, Canada and France were patrolling the streets of Port-au-Prince. This action by the Security Council was widely interpreted as endorsing whatever role the United States may have played in the removal of the former president. Yet the resolution was carefully worded to be entirely neutral on the issue. Although it expressly invoked Chapter VII, the resolution simply 'took note' of Aristide's resignation, 'acknowledged' the new president's request for urgent assistance and 'determined' that the situation 'constituted a threat to international peace and security, and to stability in the Caribbean especially through the potential outflow of people to other States in the subregion'. The invocation of Chapter VII conveniently circumvented any need to determine whether the new president was in fact legally capable of inviting an intervention.

A similar overlap of Chapter VII authorization and an invitation to intervene had occurred five years earlier in East Timor. Indonesia, under the dictatorship of President Suharto, had invaded and occupied the neighbouring Portuguese colony in December 1975. Some 200,000 East Timorese – one quarter of the population – died as a result of the invasion. The UN Security Council responded by unanimously adopting Resolution 384, in which it recognized the 'inalienable right of the people of East Timor to self-determination and independence' and deplored the 'intervention of the armed forces of Indonesia'. The Security Council called upon Indonesia to withdraw its forces and refused to recognize its claims to sovereignty over the territory. At the same time, however, the Council refused to categorize the invasion as a violation of the UN Charter, impose economic sanctions, or authorize the use of military force. Indonesia was simply too strategically important to the United States and its allies during the Cold War to be subjected to the full range of Security Council pressures.

The Suharto regime finally collapsed in 1998, and B. J. Habibie was appointed president of Indonesia. In January 1999, Habibie, in response to international pressure and in order to consolidate his power, announced a referendum whereby East Timor would choose between independence and a largely autonomous position within Indonesia. In May 1999, Indonesia and Portugal, with help from UN Secretary General Kofi Annan, concluded an agreement on the logistics of the vote, which inadvisably assigned responsibility for security during the referendum to Indonesia rather than the United Nations.

In June 1999, the Security Council dispatched an election-monitoring mission to East Timor. The mission was subsequently expanded and its mandate strengthened after disturbances by members of the pro-Indonesian militia delayed the vote. The referendum was finally held on 30 August 1999. An overwhelming majority of East Timorese – 78.5 per cent of them, out of a 97.5 per cent voter turnout – cast ballots in favour of independence. In response, the pro-Indonesian militia turned increasingly violent, killing more than a thousand people and driving hundreds of thousands from their homes. United Nations officials also came under attack and were evacuated to Australia.

Two weeks later, the United States persuaded Habibie to accept international peacekeepers. On 15 September 1999, the UN Security Council adopted Resolution 1264, a Chapter VII resolution that identified the situation in East Timor as a 'threat to peace and security'. The resolution authorized the establishment of a 9,000-strong multinational force under Australian command to 'take all necessary measures' to restore peace and security and protect and support the monitoring mission. Later, the Security Council again exercised its Chapter VII powers to establish a United Nations Transition Administration in East Timor (UNTAET) to exercise full executive and legislative authority over the territory. This was the first time the United Nations had assumed complete control over the sovereign functions of a country. Thanks to the Council's willingness to interpret its own powers broadly, and the Australian-led intervention it had authorized, East Timor achieved independence on 20 May 2002, one month after former rebel leader Xanana Gusmao was elected its first president.

From a strictly legal perspective, Habibie's consent to the peacekeeping operation meant that the Security Council's authorization was unnecessary. United Nations peacekeeping often occurs with the consent of the host country and at the initiative of the General Assembly rather than Security Council. Still, the invocation of Chapter VII meant that the legitimacy of Australia's deployment of troops into a neighbouring developing country was beyond question. The Security Council's involvement in East Timor in 1999 also closed an important circle, for the crisis was as much about Indonesia's 1975 invasion and occupation of the territory – a classic violation of Article 2(4) of the UN Charter – as it was about self-determination, human rights and democracy. Although the international community took much longer to react to the Indonesian invasion than to Iraq's seizure of Kuwait in 1990, both outcomes confirm that the conquest of territory remains intolerable both politically and in law.

*

The most recent challenge facing the UN Security Council concerns Sudan, Africa's largest country, where a major humanitarian crisis arose in 2004. In the western region of Darfur (which is roughly the size of France), some 1.8 million people were forced from their homes and villages. More than 130,000 people fled across the border into Chad and, as of December 2004, more than 70,000 people had died, with hundreds of thousands more facing disease and possible starvation.

The agents of this disaster were the 'Janjaweed', which translates roughly as 'devils on horseback with guns'. These men are members of nomadic Arab tribes that, in recent decades, have come into conflict with Darfur's black (though also Muslim) agricultural tribes as drought and growing populations increased competition for water and pasture. After some of the black tribes attempted to rise up against the Sudanese government in February 2003, Khartoum armed the Janjaweed and delegated them the task of suppressing the rebellion.

The Arabs took up their mission with a vengeance, pillaging and burning villages, shooting the men and boys and systematically beating and raping the women. The atrocities violated international humanitarian law, as codified in Common Article 3 of the 1949 Geneva Conventions (see Chapter 5). They were also actively supported by the government in Khartoum: Sudanese soldiers often accompanied the Janjaweed and military planes bombed the villages in advance of the attacks. The government also seized every opportunity to impede any significant humanitarian response, denying the seriousness of the problem and delaying supplies and entry papers for aid workers.

In June 2004, US Secretary of State Colin Powell visited a refugee camp in Darfur. At the time, Powell said that his trip was intended to prompt the international community into increasing pressure on Khartoum. The following month, the US Congress passed a resolution that identified the atrocities being committed in Darfur as 'genocide'. However, the credibility of the United States had been compromised by its actions elsewhere. When

Sudan was re-elected as a member of the UN Commission on Human Rights in May 2004, the US representative declared that an 'absurdity' had occurred and walked out of the meeting. The Sudanese representative countered that America was simply shedding 'crocodile tears', pointing to an apparent revenge attack by US forces against civilians in Fallujah, Iraq, in April 2004, and the Abu Ghraib prisoner abuse scandal. There may be some truth in this characterization of the US position as both hypocritical and insincere. In July 2004, reports surfaced that British Prime Minister Tony Blair had ordered his officials to begin planning for an armed intervention in Darfur, until Secretary of State Powell deemed the idea 'premature'.

Instead, on 30 July 2004, the UN Security Council adopted Resolution 1556. The Council began by expressing its 'grave concern at the ongoing humanitarian crisis and widespread human rights violations' as well as its 'determination to do everything possible to halt a humanitarian catastrophe'. The Council deemed the situation a 'threat to international peace and security', explicitly invoked Chapter VII, and imposed an arms embargo on the Janjaweed – a move destined to be ineffective, given that the region was already awash with small arms and has porous borders with Libya, Chad and the Central African Republic, where such weapons are readily available.

In the most important paragraph of Resolution 1556, the Council:

> *Demands* that the Government of Sudan fulfil its commitments to disarm the Janjaweed militias and apprehend and bring to justice Janjaweed leaders and their associates who have incited and carried out human rights and international humanitarian law violations and other atrocities, and *further requests* the Secretary-General to report in 30 days, and monthly thereafter, to the Council on the progress or lack thereof by the Government of Sudan on this matter and *expresses its intention* to consider further actions, including measures as provided for

in Article 41 of the Charter of the United Nations on the Government of Sudan, in the event of non-compliance.

Although the word 'sanctions' was dropped from the resolution under pressure from China, Pakistan and Russia, the resolution did refer to Article 41, which gives the UN Security Council authority to order a 'complete or partial interruption of economic relations'. Yet most economic measures would not have much effect against Khartoum, which is already subject to US sanctions as an alleged state sponsor of terrorism. An oil embargo could have a significant impact, but China and Russia would block any attempt to impose this particular penalty. Both these veto-holding permanent members of the Security Council invested heavily in Sudan's oil industry after Western companies withdrew their operations when Khartoum's human rights record came under public scrutiny. For this reason, there is also little prospect that the Security Council will use Chapter VII to authorize the use of military force in Sudan.

The only international organization to have taken significant action in the region has been the African Union (AU), which in August 2004 sent a force of 300 Rwandan and Nigerian troops to protect 100 peace-observers already in Darfur. The AU subsequently prepared to send some 3,000 additional soldiers, while the United States, Canada and European Union indicated their willingness to provide logistical and financial support. But in the absence of authorization by the UN Security Council, the deployment of these forces is dependent on Khartoum's co-operation and consent, which has only reluctantly been forthcoming.

France, concerned about the destabilizing effect on neighbouring Chad of hundreds of thousands of refugees and cross-border incursions by the Janjaweed, sent 200 soldiers to the eastern territory of the former French colony with the consent of the government in N'Djaména. In early September 2004, the United States submitted a draft resolution to the UN Security Council that would have imposed an oil embargo on Sudan, while

Secretary of State Colin Powell and President George W. Bush both declared that genocide had occurred there. But there was still no agreement within the Security Council, or any willingness on the part of the US government to intervene militarily. The only country ready to stand up directly to the Janjaweed, and through them Sudan, was Rwanda. Although Rwandan troops are currently committing their own atrocities in the eastern Congo, Kigali still carries considerable moral weight on the issue of genocide. As he inspected the 155 Rwandan soldiers before their departure for Darfur in August 2004, President Paul Kagame said:

> Our forces will not stand by and watch innocent civilians being hacked to death like was the case here in 1994. I have no doubt that they certainly will intervene and use force to protect civilians. In my view, it does not make sense to provide security to peace observers while the local population is left to die.

If only the permanent members of the UN Security Council had displayed similar candour and courage. On 18 November 2004, during a special meeting of the Council in Nairobi, Kenya, UN Secretary General Kofi Annan reported that 'the security situation in Darfur continues to deteriorate'. The Council responded by adopting a third resolution that, again, only hinted at unspecified action if the hostilities in Darfur continued.

The extension of the Security Council's competence to authorize mandatory sanctions and forceful action for humanitarian purposes has changed international law for the better, providing for the possibility of humanitarian intervention in a manner that is consistent with the existing rules on recourse to force. Yet the Security Council remains a political body that cannot itself be forced to act. Frequently, it will not take action, even when – as in Darfur – the moral case is overwhelming. This raises the question of what, if anything, should be done in such circumstances – a question that is considered at length in Part III of this book.

3

Implied Authorization and Intentional Ambiguity

In April 1991, Saddam Hussein's forces began a campaign of retribution in northern Iraq, after the Kurds of that region – at the apparent encouragement of President George H. W. Bush – had attempted an uprising during the 1991 Gulf War. In response, the United States, Britain, France, Italy and the Netherlands deployed forces and established so-called 'safe havens' for civilians in northern Iraq. The five intervening countries sought to justify their action – codenamed 'Operation Provide Comfort' – on the basis of a UN Security Council resolution adopted on 5 April 1991. In Resolution 688, the Security Council expressed grave concern at 'the repression of the Iraqi civilian population... including most recently in Kurdish-populated areas, which led to a massive flow of refugees towards and across international frontiers and to cross-border incursions, which threaten international peace and security'. The Council also called on countries to aid humanitarian relief efforts to be organized by then UN Secretary General Javier Perez de Cuellar.

Resolution 688 did not expressly authorize the use of force. China, concerned about the Security Council reaching into the domestic affairs of sovereign states, had reportedly threatened to veto any resolution that would authorize military action to protect the Kurds. Within a few weeks, more than a million refugees had either crossed, or were attempting to cross, from Iraq into Iran and Turkey. Television footage of hundreds of thousands of desperate people trapped in frigid mountain passes resonated with the Western public, and this in turn prompted the governments of the United States, Britain, France, Italy and the Netherlands to declare all Iraqi territory north of the 36th parallel out of bounds to Iraqi armed forces. They argued that this move was 'in support of' Resolution 688.

Later, the United States, Britain and France transformed the northern exclusion zone into two 'no-fly' zones: one north of the 36th parallel, the other south of the 32nd parallel. The southern 'no-fly' zone was created to protect Shiites who had similarly attempted an uprising against Saddam Hussein. Both 'no-fly' zones were justified primarily on the basis of Security Council Resolution 688, again despite the apparent absence of any words of authorization in the resolution. The justification was properly questioned by other countries and, in 1996, France pulled out of the operation after the United States and Britain extended the southern zone northwards to just south of Baghdad. But, given the power and influence of the United States and the unpopularity of Saddam Hussein, there was little more that other governments could – or wished to – do. At least Washington and London were advancing a legal argument based tenuously on Resolution 688, rather than simply disregarding the law.

Only some UN Security Council resolutions authorize the use of force unequivocally. Resolution 678, adopted in November 1990 following the Iraqi invasion of Kuwait, was one such resolution, authorizing UN member states 'to use all necessary means...to restore international peace and security to the area'. Other resolutions, such as Resolution 688, are considerably less clear. Security Council resolutions are sometimes worded ambiguously as a result of rushed negotiations; in other instances, the ambiguity is the result of deliberate compromise. In either case, some countries will sometimes argue that force has implicitly been authorized, while others will adamantly maintain the opposite view.

In 1997, the Federal Republic of Yugoslavia, headed by President Slobodan Milošević, launched a brutal crackdown on a rebel militia army and its supporters in the primarily Muslim province of Kosovo. Within a year, UN Secretary General Kofi Annan reported that force was being used in an 'indiscriminate and disproportionate' manner against civilians and that 'appalling atrocities' were being committed.

The UN Security Council responded on 23 September 1998 by adopting Resolution 1199. Acting expressly under Chapter VII, the Council demanded that the Milošević government cease its 'repressive actions against the peaceful population' of Kosovo and resolve the situation by non-forceful means. The Council also warned that, if Milošević failed to comply, it would 'consider further action and additional measures to maintain or restore peace and security in the region'.

One month later, the Security Council adopted Resolution 1203 in which it welcomed an agreement between Belgrade and the Organization for Security and Cooperation in Europe (OSCE) that provided for the establishment of a peace verification mission in Kosovo. The Security Council emphasized the need to ensure the safety and security of the members of the OSCE mission and affirmed that the situation in Kosovo remained a threat to peace and security. Then, acting expressly under Chapter VII, the Council stated that 'in the event of an emergency, action may be needed to ensure their [the members of the mission's] safety and freedom of movement'. The Council hinted at a possible need to intervene to rescue the OSCE personnel but said nothing more that could be construed as authorizing military action. The Council also decided to 'remain seized of the matter'.

On 24 March 1999, without the adoption of a further UN Security Council resolution, NATO began an air campaign against targets, not only in Kosovo but also in Serbia and Montenegro. Very little was advanced in the way of legal justification for the air strikes, though most of the countries involved considered it relevant that the Security Council had identified the situation in Kosovo as a threat to peace and security in both Resolutions 1199 and 1203. To the degree most of the intervening powers provided a justification at all, they argued that, once the Security Council has identified a threat and demanded action from a 'problem' state, the members of the United Nations are implicitly entitled to ensure that the Council's will is carried out. The Kosovo War was condemned as illegal by Russia, China and a large number of developing countries. And so, while an implied authorization argument was floated during the Kosovo War, very few people – even those who advanced the argument – took it all that seriously.

The march towards removing Saddam Hussein from power began shortly after George W. Bush entered the White House in January 2001. There were multiple, overlapping motivations for going to war, including concerns about Iraqi weapons of mass destruction, political instability in the Middle East, access to oil, and a personal vendetta arising from Saddam's failed attempt to assassinate the president's father, former president George H. W. Bush, in Kuwait in 1993.

Two legal justifications were advanced for the 2003 invasion. The sole argument advanced by Britain and Australia, and the main argument advanced by the United States, is examined here. The second justification, an extended claim to pre-emptive self-defence, is considered at length in Chapter 6.

The first justification for the military intervention in Iraq returns to Resolution 678, adopted by the UN Security Council following Iraq's invasion of Kuwait in 1990, whereby it authorized UN member states to 'use all necessary means...to restore peace and security to the area'. The argument claims, essentially, that the authorization provided by Resolution 678 was suspended – not terminated – by the ceasefire imposed by Resolution 687 in April 1991. This suspended authorization could be reactivated – so the argument goes – if and when Iraq engaged in a 'material breach' of its ceasefire and disarmament obligations. The concept of material breach, drawn from the law of treaties, had been expressly endorsed by the Security Council in the context of Iraq, most notably in the unanimously adopted Resolution 1441 of 8 November 2002, which found Iraq in material breach. This resolution gave Iraq 'a final opportunity to comply with its disarmament obligations' and warned that non-compliance would have 'serious consequences'. Iraq's failure to cooperate fully, including during February and March 2003, when it refused to allow weapons scientists to be interviewed outside the country, was argued to constitute a further material breach of Resolution 687, thereby permitting enforced compliance. The argument concludes with the assertion that, had the Security Council thought that an additional resolution was necessary before military action could be taken, it would have spelled out this requirement in Resolution 1441.

This approach, coupling the concept of material breach with that of implied authorization, is countered by several good arguments. For example, the 1991 ceasefire resolution is clearly worded to terminate – not suspend – the previous year's authorization of military force. In any event, since the parties to the ceasefire were the UN Security Council and Iraq, the coalition countries involved in the ejection of the Iraqis from Kuwait were not parties to the ceasefire (though they were bound by it). Any material breach could not have reactivated a right for the coalition members to use force independently. Moreover, Resolution 1441 neither specified the legal consequences of material breach nor expressly authorized military action. Indeed, following its adoption, all the Security Council's members, including the United States and Britain, confirmed publicly that the resolution provided no 'automaticity' – by which they presumably meant that force could not be used until a further resolution was adopted.

Disagreements over the legality of the Iraq War attracted unprecedented media attention, especially in the United Kingdom. Breaking with tradition, the holders of the Cambridge and Oxford chairs in international law, James Crawford and Vaughan Lowe, took a public stance against the British government. Even more telling was the resignation of Elisabeth Wilmshurst, the deputy legal adviser to the British Foreign Office. Her boss, Michael Wood, stoically remained in place and subsequently received a knighthood.

But the fact of the matter is that the members of the UN Security Council had agreed to disagree when, in November 2002, they adopted Resolution 1441. Different provisions of that resolution provided support to both sides of the debate over the legality of going to war against Iraq. By carefully balancing the arguments, the Security Council succeeded in effectively de-legalizing the situation, and thus protecting the international legal system from the damage that would otherwise have resulted when politics prevailed. In particular, the inclusion of language in favour of a right to go to war provided the United States with an argument – the material breach argument – that was more legally tenable than its parallel claim of a extended right of pre-emptive self-defence. And that more tenable argument then had the effect of absorbing much of the impact that the pre-emption claim might have had as a precedent in customary international law – a precedent that, had it been established, would have been of great concern to European and developing states. Most journalists, and many international lawyers, were woefully inattentive to this crucial context to the legal debate.

Yet the debate over the legality of the 2003 Iraq War went deeper than contesting political positions supported by an intentionally ambiguous UN Security Council resolution. At a more fundamental level, the debate concerned competing methods of legal interpretation and, more specifically, which particular approach should be taken to interpreting Security Council resolutions.

Most international lawyers regard the law through a judicial prism; courts must render a clear decision on the arguments presented. International lawyers therefore tend to believe that a right answer is always to be found. For their answers, they look to the 'sources' of international law, including treaties, customary international law and, since 1945, UN Security Council resolutions adopted under Chapter VII of the UN Charter. Where gaps exist, either in the source material or the application of the material to a specific dispute, international lawyers seek to fill them through analogies to established precedents, rules and principles.

But the analogies chosen and the weight accorded to source materials remain somewhat discretionary and, as a result, different international lawyers may assess the sources slightly differently. Nowhere was the impact of such subtle differences of approach more apparent than during the debates in early 2003 over the interpretation of UN Security Council Resolution 1441.

Although the members of the Security Council were aware that the ambiguities of Resolution 1441 provided room for argument on both sides of the debate over whether war would be legal, each believed that their particular understanding of the resolution was legally correct. Compared to most other countries, the United States tends to place more weight on the 'object and purpose' of international documents and less weight on their actual terms. This tendency dates back to at least 1968 when the US delegation to the Vienna Conference on the Law of Treaties proposed a purposive approach to treaty interpretation that emphasized a comprehensive examination of the context of any particular treaty, so as to ascertain the common will of the parties – as that will evolved over time. This approach was rejected overwhelmingly by the other countries at the conference. Accordingly, Article 31(1) of the Vienna Convention stipulates: 'A treaty shall be interpreted in good faith in accordance with the ordinary meaning to be given to the terms of the treaty in their context and in the light of its object and purpose', with the emphasis being on ordinary meaning. As importantly, Article 32 of the Vienna Convention restricts consideration of the 'preparatory work of the treaty...to determine the meaning' to situations where 'the interpretation according to Article 31' has left the meaning 'ambiguous or obscure' or led to a result 'which is manifestly absurd or unreasonable'. In other words, preparatory documents and records of negotiations cannot generally be used for interpretive purposes.

Despite Articles 31 and 32, the United States continues to prefer a more purposive, less textually oriented approach, most notably when interpreting the UN Charter. An extreme example of this tendency arose during the 1999 Kosovo crisis. As former State Department spokesman James Rubin explained:

> There was a series of strained telephone calls between [US Secretary of State Madeleine] Albright and [UK Foreign Secretary Robin] Cook, in which he cited problems 'with our lawyers' over using force in the absence of UN endorsement. 'Get new lawyers,' she suggested. But with a push from prime minister Tony Blair, the British finally agreed that UN security council approval was not legally required.

Unlike the UN Charter, Security Council resolutions are not treaties. Treaties resemble contracts whereas Security Council resolutions resemble executive orders, so the applicable interpretive rules may differ somewhat. Relatively little academic writing has been directed to this issue – perhaps because the Security Council was inactive for decades due to the Cold War rivalry between two veto-wielding superpowers – and those scholars who have studied it favour divergent approaches.

Before he became the Legal Adviser to the British Foreign Office, Michael Wood advanced an approach to interpreting UN Security Council resolutions that takes into account the full background of the Security Council's involvement with an issue, in order to determine the result the Council was seeking to achieve. Such a purposive approach leads relatively easily to a presumption in favour of an authorization to use force when: (1) a resolution is adopted; (2) the Security Council has previously identified a threat to international peace and security; (3) strict conditions have been placed on the threatening state, and; (4) the state has conspicuously failed to meet the conditions. Although the presumption may be countered by clear evidence to the contrary, textual ambiguities are read, where possible, in a manner consistent with the view that the Security Council intends its demands to be met and enforced. This approach was used by the United States and Britain to interpret Resolution 1441 on Iraq, as well as the resolutions adopted with regard to northern Iraq in 1991 and Kosovo in 1998.

In sharp contrast, Jochen Frowein, the recently retired director of the Max Planck Institute for International Law in Heidelberg, Germany, has advocated an interpretive approach to Security Council resolutions that is more restrictive than the approach taken to treaties. Frowein discounts the relevance of the subjective intentions of Security Council members, since any country against which Chapter VII power is wielded is unlikely to have contributed to the resolution's formulation. This means that: 'As far as they are concerned the resolution has the same sort of objective existence as laws or administrative acts in a specific legal system. Therefore, the objective view of the neutral observer as addressee must be the most important aspect for the interpretation.' Frowein even suggests that the non-participation of the countries subject to resolutions, when combined with the Security Council's capacity to interfere with the territorial integrity and political independence of those same countries, requires a presumption that sovereign rights have neither been surrendered nor removed. The result is an approach to the interpretation of Security Council resolutions that focuses narrowly on the ordinary meaning of the terms.

The disagreement over the legality of the 2003 Iraq War indicated that many governments subscribe to the more textually oriented approach advanced by Frowein. The approach, modelled on Article 31 of the Vienna Convention of the Law of Treaties, correctly holds that the UN Security Council only means what it specifically says. There is, consequently, an interpretive presumption against the authorization of military force.

In the aftermath of the Iraq War, the damning failure of US-led weapons inspectors to find evidence that Saddam Hussein posed an imminent threat weakened the claim, not that Resolution 1441 authorized the use of force, but that any such authorization was appropriately relied upon by the United States and Britain. Similarly, the reluctance of many countries to support the US-led occupation and reconstruction of Iraq confirms that Washington and London's interpretation of Resolution 1441 was not widely shared. That said, governments are now exercising greater caution when negotiating and adopting UN Security Council resolutions. Resolution 1483 on Iraq, adopted in May 2003, was worded very tightly in order to leave little room for arguments that it provided retroactive authorization for the war. The same is true of Resolution 1511, adopted in October 2003, even though this resolution authorized a US-led multilateral force to provide 'security and stability' in Iraq. The attempt to advance a purposive approach to the interpretation of Security Council resolutions has backfired, prompting clarity in drafting and objectivity in interpretation. As a result, the textual approach to the interpretation of Security Council resolutions is well on its way to achieving the status of widely accepted, universally binding customary international law.

This does not mean, however, that the United States has given up on this legal battle. In a September 2004 interview with the BBC World Service, Secretary General Kofi Annan expressed the opinion that the Iraq War was 'illegal' since 'it was up to the Security Council to approve or determine' what the 'consequences should be' for Iraq's non-compliance with previously adopted resolutions. The White House immediately expressed its strong disagreement with this influential assessment. It then stood quietly by while a group of Republican Congressmen demanded Annan's resignation over the 'oil-for-food' scandal, whereby Saddam Hussein had abused an UN-run programme designed to provide humanitarian essentials to civilians in Iraq while the country was subject to Security Council sanctions. When pressed by reporters about the matter in November 2004, John Danforth, the US ambassador to the United Nations, pointedly declined to express confidence in the Secretary General's leadership. In the world of diplomatic protocol, this amounted to a powerful attack; it also suggested that, behind closed doors, the United States was pressing for Annan's departure before the end of his second term in 2006. Such is the extent of the Bush Administration's intolerance of dissent about the wisdom and legality of its actions.

Part Two

Self-defence

4

'Inherent Right' of Self-defence

In 1837, the British were crushing a rebellion in Upper Canada (now Ontario). The United States, while unwilling to antagonize a superpower by supporting the rebels directly, did not prevent a private militia from being formed in upstate New York. The 'volunteers' used a steamboat, the *Caroline*, to transport arms and men to the rebel headquarters on Navy Island, on the Canadian side of the Niagara River. The British responded with a night raid, capturing the vessel as it was docked at Fort Schlosser, New York. They set the boat on fire and sent it over Niagara Falls. Two men were killed as they fled the steamer and two prisoners were taken back to Canada but later released.

The incident caused disquiet in Washington. British forces, having torched the White House and Capitol Building in 1814, were again intervening on US territory. Secretary of State Forsyth wrote a letter to the British minister at Washington, one Mr Fox, asserting that the incident had produced 'the most painful emotions of surprise and regret'. The minister responded that the destruction of the *Caroline* was an act of 'necessary self-defence' – though probably all he meant by this statement was that the act was justified on political grounds. Historically, self-defence had been a political justification for what, from a legal perspective, were ordinary acts of war. The consent-based international law of the early nineteenth century rejected natural law distinctions between just and unjust wars.

The dispute over the destruction of the *Caroline* was settled in 1842 following a change of administration in Washington and the delegation of a new British minister, Lord Ashburton, to the

United States. Lord Ashburton was extremely well connected in Washington – his wife was the daughter of a US senator – and the diplomacy that followed was carefully managed on both sides.

Daniel Webster, the new Secretary of State, began by conceding that the use of force in self-defence could be justified in some circumstances:

> Undoubtedly it is just, that, while it is admitted that exceptions growing out of the great law of self-defence do exist, those exceptions should be confined to cases in which the necessity of that self-defence is instant, overwhelming, leaving no choice of means, and no moment of deliberation.

Webster then added, importantly, that nothing 'unreasonable or excessive' could be done in self-defence.

Other governments subsequently accepted these criteria – 'necessity and proportionality' – as the parameters of a new customary international law right of self-defence. Thus, while the case of the *Caroline* did nothing to prevent further aggression, it did lead to a legal distinction between war and self-defence. As long as a military response met the 'necessity and proportionality' criteria and the act defended against was not an act of war, peace would be maintained; a matter of considerable importance to relatively weak countries, as the United States then was.

Another century and the First World War were required to convince statesmen of the need for legal constraints on military aggression. A first effort was made in 1919 when the Covenant of the League of Nations was adopted at Versailles. Under the Covenant, the Council of the League could issue recommendations to countries that seemed to be heading for war. But if the members of the Council failed to agree, the disputing governments were free to take whatever action they considered 'necessary for the maintenance of right and justice'. The League of Nations also lacked the capacity to enforce its recommendations. Any hope that the League would coordinate enforcement action among its members disappeared in 1920, when the US Senate withheld its consent to the ratification of the Covenant of the League of Nations.

The Kellogg–Briand Pact of 1928 prohibited 'recourse to war for the solution of international controversies'. The Pact, named after US Secretary of State Frank Kellogg and French Foreign Minister Aristide Briand, was initially signed by fifteen countries and eventually ratified by sixty-two. However, like the League of Nations Covenant, the Kellogg–Briand Pact lacked an enforcement mechanism and had little practical effect. Some countries, such as Italy when it invaded Abyssinia and Japan when it invaded Manchuria, evaded their obligations under the Pact simply by avoiding formal declarations of war.

The Kellogg–Briand Pact also included a side agreement between the United States and France that provided an exception for self-defence. Neither the nature of the right nor the instances in which it could be invoked were defined. When the US Senate voted 85–1 in favour of ratifying the Pact, it did so on the explicit understanding that it did not imperil the Monroe Doctrine: President James Monroe's 1823 declaration that any European interference in the Western hemisphere would be regarded as a threat to the security of the United States. Given these complexities, the customary international law criteria established during the *Caroline* incident remained the only discernible legal constraints on the recourse to force in international affairs.

In 1945, the UN Charter required all countries to 'refrain...from the threat or use of force'. By using the general term 'use of force', the Charter extended the prohibition on war to include undeclared armed conflicts. The Charter also created the UN Security Council and gave it authority to determine 'the existence of any threat to the peace, breach of the peace or act of aggression', impose sanctions, and 'take such action by air, sea or land forces as may be necessary'. But the drafters of the Charter were hardly naive. Recognizing that the existence of the United Nations could be imperilled if powerful countries were subjected to the threat of collective action, they granted permanent membership on the Security Council and a veto over its resolutions to Britain, China, France, the Soviet Union and United States. Mindful that the Security Council could never respond promptly to every act of aggression, they also included an exception for force used in self-defence. This time, the exception was not left undefined. In addition to the customary international law criteria of 'necessity and proportionality', three further restrictions were introduced: 1) a state could act in self-defence only if subject to an 'armed attack'; 2) acts of self-defence had to be reported immediately to the Security Council; and 3) the right to respond would terminate as soon as the Council took action. The relevant provision of the UN Charter is Article 51:

> Nothing in the present Charter shall impair the inherent right of individual or collective self-defence if an armed attack occurs against a Member of the United Nations, until the Security Council has taken measures necessary to maintain international peace and security. Measures taken by Members in the exercise of this right of self-defence shall be immediately reported to the Security Council and shall not in any way affect the authority and responsibility of the Security Council under the present Charter to take at any time such action as it deems necessary in order to maintain or restore international peace and security.

Despite this careful attempt at definition, the content of Article 51 is greatly informed by customary international law, in part because of the explicit reference to the 'inherent' character of the right of self-defence. And so, while the right is codified in an almost universally ratified treaty, its contours have gradually evolved – or at least become more easily discernible – as the result of state practice and expressions of *opinio juris* since 1945. For example, it is not clear from the ordinary meaning or context of Article 51 that armed attacks against a country's citizens *outside* its territory constitute attacks against a 'Member of the United

Nations' sufficient to trigger the right to self-defence. This particular ambiguity was resolved in 1976.

On 27 June 1976, an Air France jet left Israel for France with 251 passengers and a crew of twelve on board. After a brief stop in Athens, pro-Palestinian hijackers seized control of the plane and forced it to land in Entebbe, Uganda. The hijackers threatened to kill the hostages unless 53 pro-Palestinian terrorists were released from jails in France, Israel, Kenya, Switzerland and West Germany. On the third day of the hijacking, forty-seven non-Jewish passengers were released. On the fourth day another 100 were let go. The Government of Uganda, led by the dictator Idi Amin, took no apparent steps to secure the release of the remaining, mostly Israeli, passengers or the crew.

On 3 July 1976, shortly before the deadline set by the hijackers, Israeli commandos conducted an audacious and highly successful rescue operation. Without notifying the Ugandan government, a small force landed at Entebbe airport, stormed the plane and killed the hijackers. They saved the lives of all but three of the hostages and flew them back to Israel. Jonathan Netanyahu, the leader of the commando unit and the brother of Israeli politician Binyamin Netanyahu, was the only Israeli soldier to die in the raid. A number of Ugandan soldiers were also killed and several Ugandan military aircraft destroyed.

Israel claimed that international law allowed it to use force to protect its nationals abroad when the country in which they had fallen into danger was unable or unwilling to do so. Two draft resolutions were introduced in the UN Security Council. The first, prepared by Britain and the United States, condemned the hijacking and called on states to prevent and punish all such terrorist attacks. This resolution was put to a vote but failed to obtain the nine out of fifteen votes necessary. Two countries (Panama and Romania) formally abstained from the vote, while seven (Benin, China, Guyana, Libya, Pakistan, the Soviet Union and Tanzania) refused even to participate.

The second draft resolution, submitted by Benin, Libya and Tanzania, condemned the violation of Uganda's sovereignty and territorial integrity and demanded that Israel pay compensation for all damage caused. The resolution was never put to a vote. The response of countries outside the Security Council was similarly mixed and muted, signalling widespread, tacit acceptance of the Israeli claim. Today, the Entebbe incident is regarded as having decisively contributed to a limited extension of the right of self-defence in international affairs to include the protection of nationals abroad. When civil strife threatens foreign nationals, whether in Haiti, Liberia or Sierra Leone, sending soldiers to rescue them has become so commonplace that the issue of legality is rarely raised. When controversy does arise, as when France intervened to rescue nationals in Mauritania (1977), Gabon (1990), Rwanda (1990), Chad (1992) and the Central African Republic (1996), concerns usually focus on whether the intervening government has exceeded the criteria of necessity and proportionality – for example, by using the protection of nationals as a pretence for intervening in a civil war.

If the right of self-defence extends to the protection of nationals abroad, what then of situations where an armed attack has occurred but the immediate threat has passed? In other words, is self-defence limited to the warding off of attacks-in-progress or does the right extend to action taken in response to a recent attack? If so, what, if any, line is to be drawn between defensive and punitive armed responses?

In April 1993, an attempt to assassinate former US President George H. W. Bush was thwarted when a sophisticated car bomb was discovered in Kuwait. Two months later, the United States fired twenty-three Tomahawk cruise missiles at the Iraqi Military Intelligence Headquarters in Baghdad. Sixteen of the missiles hit the target. Some six to eight people were killed.

Madeleine Albright, who was the US ambassador to the United Nations at the time, presented evidence of the Iraqi government's involvement in the assassination attempt to the UN Security Council. She asserted that the attempt to kill the former president was 'a direct attack on the United States, an attack that required a direct United States response'. Moreover, Albright claimed, the response was permitted under Article 51 of the Charter.

The US claim was unusual in several respects. First, the United States had not been attacked, nor was the assassination attempt aimed at a group of Americans. The car bomb was directed against a single citizen while he was outside the United States. Of course, George H. W. Bush is no ordinary citizen: even the Democrat Clinton Administration of the day regarded the former Republican president as a symbol and projection of US sovereignty when he travelled abroad.

Second, the armed response took place two months after the assassination attempt had been foiled and the threat to the former president eliminated. The response, rather than being an act of self-defence as such, was directed at the dual goals of punishing Iraq and deterring future plots. The missile strike therefore seemed more in the nature of a reprisal than an act of self-defence. But reprisals have been illegal under international law since the adoption of the UN Charter of 1945. In 1964, the UN Security Council went so far as to adopt a resolution that condemned armed reprisals as 'incompatible with the purposes and principles of the United Nations'. In response, some countries, including the United States, have persistently sought to extend the right of self-defence to include acts designed more to punish than defend.

In this instance, the members of the Security Council responded favourably to the US action and its claim of self-defence. Japan said that the use of force was an 'unavoidable situation'. Germany described the strike as a 'justified response'. Outside the Security Council, overall reaction was less favourable. Iran and Libya condemned the strike as an act of aggression, while the Arab League expressed 'extreme regret' and said that force should only have been used if authorized by the Security Council.

Determining whether an action falls within the rubric of self-defence will usually turn on the facts of the specific situation. In the case of the foiled 1993 assassination attempt, the US government explained that it had taken two months to gather conclusive evidence of Iraqi involvement in the plot and, once it was certain that Iraq was responsible, it had wasted no time in acting. The British found themselves in a similar situation in 1982, when an immediate response to Argentina's invasion of the Falklands was precluded by the time it took to assemble and send a naval task force from the United Kingdom to the South Atlantic, though the continued Argentine occupation of the islands could also have been considered an ongoing armed attack.

Still, once an armed attack has come and gone and there is no continuing or immediate threat, there is nothing to stop the country that has been attacked from asking the UN Security Council to respond. In most domestic legal systems, the right of self-defence terminates the moment an attack has ceased and there is time to call the police. However, since the Security Council is a political body, the country that has been attacked cannot be certain that the Council will respond to its pleas. The extension of the right of self-defence to the period following an attack represents a pragmatic response, not just to the prohibition of reprisals in international affairs but also to the unreliability of the Security Council as a policing mechanism for the international rules on the use of military force.

That said, this pragmatic extension of self-defence to the period following an attack exacerbates the very obstacle it seeks to overcome. By expanding the scope of situations where countries can use force without Security Council authorization, any extension to the right of self-defence necessarily decreases the frequency with which the Council is called upon to act. The United States, by pushing for this and other extensions to the right of self-defence, not only increases its own freedom to act, it diminishes the role and authority of the United Nations. Pragmatism can be attractive, but it carries a price.

5

Self-defence against Terrorism

On 11 September 2001, nineteen al-Qaeda operatives seized four passenger jets, crashing two of them into the World Trade Center and another into the Pentagon; the fourth plane was brought down in a field in Pennsylvania after the passengers revolted against the hijackers. Nearly 3,000 people were killed in the attacks. Almost immediately, the US government declared that it would respond militarily on the basis of self-defence. But as a legal justification for the use of force in Afghanistan – the country harbouring and supporting the al-Qaeda leadership – the right of self-defence was not as suitable as it might at first have seemed.

Even when countries are directly implicated in terrorism, acts of self-defence directed against them have not attracted much international support. In April 1986, a terrorist bomb exploded in a West Berlin nightclub crowded with US servicemen. Two soldiers and a Turkish woman were killed and 230 people were wounded, including fifty US military personnel. Ten days later, the United States responded by bombing a number of targets in Tripoli. More than fifteen people were killed, including an adopted daughter of Libyan leader Muammar Qaddafi.

The US government claimed the strike on Tripoli was legally justified as an act of self-defence. As then Secretary of State George P. Shultz said:

> [T]he Charter's restrictions on the use or threat of force in international relations include a specific exception for the right of self-defence. It is absurd to argue that international law prohibits us from capturing terrorists in international waters or

airspace; from attacking them on the soil of other nations, even for the purpose of rescuing hostages; or from using force against states that support, train, and harbour terrorists or guerrillas.

Yet the US claim was widely rejected, with many governments also expressing doubt as to whether the attack on Libya met the 'necessity and proportionality' requirements for self-defence. The most significant evidence of state practice and *opinio juris* in this instance was the refusal of France and Spain – both NATO allies of the United States – to allow their airspace to be used by the bombers that conducted the raid. As a result, the pilots, who began their mission at a US airbase in Britain, had to fly westwards around the Iberian Peninsula. The detour necessitated the heightened risk of mid-air refuelling. Denying the use of airspace is highly unusual, especially among allies. Canada, France and Germany opposed the 2003 Iraq War but left their airspace open to US military aircraft – including ultra long-range B-2 bombers – flying to and from the Middle East.

Today, the additional question arises as to whether the right of self-defence extends to situations where military responses take place on the territory of countries not directly implicated in the terrorist acts. For decades, the United States, Israel and apartheid South Africa advanced precisely this claim. Israel, for instance, claimed to be acting in self-defence when it attacked the headquarters of the Palestine Liberation Organization in Tunisia in 1985. The UN Security Council condemned the action, with the United States, unusually, abstaining rather than vetoing the resolution. A number of governments expressed concern that the territorial integrity of a sovereign state had been violated in an attempt to target, not the state itself, but alleged terrorists present there.

On 7 August 1998, powerful bombs exploded outside the US embassies in Nairobi, Kenya and Dar es Salaam, Tanzania. Twelve Americans and more than 200 Kenyans and Tanzanians were killed; thousands more were injured. United States intelligence sources indicated that Osama bin Laden and his al-Qaeda organization were responsible for the attacks. Two weeks later, the United States fired seventy-nine Tomahawk cruise missiles at six terrorist training camps around the town of Khowst, Afghanistan, and at a pharmaceutical plant on the outskirts of Khartoum, Sudan. At the time, the Central Intelligence Agency (CIA) was convinced that the plant was producing precursors to chemical weapons; it subsequently emerged that the intelligence was flawed.

The US government justified its actions on the basis of self-defence. As then National Security Adviser Sandy Berger said: 'I think it is appropriate, under Article 51 of the UN Charter, for protecting the self-defence of the United States... for us to try and disrupt and destroy those kinds of military terrorist targets.' Since propriety does not necessarily coincide with legality, Berger's choice of words may indicate that he recognized the tenuous nature of the claim. The United States was not asserting that it had been attacked by Afghanistan and Sudan; instead, it was claiming the right to fire missiles into those countries in response to the actions of a group that was not a state.

In an attempt to dampen international criticism, and perhaps modify the law, President Bill Clinton telephoned Tony Blair, Jacques Chirac and German Chancellor Helmut Kohl shortly before the strikes and asked for their support. Without having time to consult their lawyers, all three leaders agreed – and subsequently made concurring public statements immediately following the US action. As a result of the timely expressions of support, other countries were more restrained in their response than they might have been. Pakistan protested strongly, which was understandable given that its airspace had been used without permission and a stray cruise missile had landed on its territory. Cuba also denounced the raid, as did Iran, Iraq, Libya and Russia, and UN Secretary General Kofi Annan diplomatically expressed 'concern'. But most governments and international organizations remained silent; indeed, the incident never even made it on to the agenda of the UN Security Council. This broad lack of response probably contributed to obfuscating the limits of self-defence, if not to changing the law as it governs recourse to force against countries that harbour or otherwise support international terrorists.

It would serve the United States' interests to have the right of self-defence extend to the use of force against terrorists abroad, there being no prospect that another country would exercise self-defence against terrorists on US territory. At the same time, however, the United States has to regularly depend on allies who value and abide by international law. On other occasions, the United States finds it convenient to deploy legal arguments when seeking to persuade other countries not to use force themselves. It is this combined need for flexibility, compliance and constraint that motivates the law-making and law-changing efforts of the United States. Whenever the US government wishes to act in a manner that is inconsistent with existing international law, its lawyers regularly and actively seek to change the law. They do so by provoking and steering changing patterns of state practice and *opinio juris*, with a view to incrementally modifying customary rules and accepted interpretations of treaties such as the UN Charter.

Bill Clinton's telephone calls to close allies immediately prior to the 1998 missile strikes on Sudan and Afghanistan are one example of an attempt to promote support and acquiescence in a US legal position, and thus to change international law. A better example, directed at generating the exact same legal change, is found in the US government's approach to international law in the aftermath of 11 September 2001. At the time, there were several legal justifications available to the United States for the use of military force in Afghanistan. First, the United States could have argued that it was acting at the invitation of the Northern Alliance, a group which still controlled a portion of the country's territory and could have been cast – albeit tenuously – as the legitimate government of Afghanistan. Invitation is widely accepted as a legal basis for intervention under customary international law, since the UN Charter's prohibition on the use of force is only directed at non-consensual interventions. Second, the United States could have sought explicit authorization for military action from the UN Security Council. Such authorization would certainly have been granted, given the widespread sympathy that existed for the United States at the time as well as the heightened concern about terrorism felt by governments everywhere. The request was never made. Even then, the United States could have argued that Security Council Resolution 1373, adopted on 28 September 2001 and directed primarily at the freezing of terrorist assets, contained language that authorized the use of military force. Third, the United States could have claimed a right of humanitarian intervention based, in part, on the precedent of the 1999 Kosovo War, because millions of Afghan lives were at risk from famine during the winter of 2001–2002.

Yet the United States chose to focus on a single justification: a right of self-defence against terrorism. In doing so, it found itself in somewhat of a legal dilemma, though not an entirely unhelpful one. In order to maintain the coalition of countries willing to use force against terrorism, the response to the 11 September 2001 attacks had to comply with the criteria of necessity and proportionality. The military action therefore had to be focused on those individuals believed responsible for the deaths of the nearly 3,000 US citizens. But if the United States had singled out bin Laden and al-Qaeda as its targets, it would have run up against the widely held view that terrorist attacks, in and of themselves, do not justify military responses within the territory of sovereign countries. Even today, most countries are wary of a rule that could expose them to attack whenever terrorists were thought to operate from within their territory. Consider, for instance, the position of Germany after 11 September 2001: although the city of Hamburg had unwittingly harboured several of the terrorists, few people would maintain that this fact alone could justify a US attack.

In response to this dilemma, the United States adopted a two-pronged legal strategy. First, it implicated the Taliban. By giving refuge to bin Laden and al-Qaeda and refusing to hand them over, the Taliban was alleged to have directly facilitated and endorsed their actions. The United States even gave the Taliban a deadline for surrendering bin Laden, a move that served to ensure their complicity. Moreover, the Taliban's continued control over Afghanistan was viewed as a threat, in and of itself, of even more terrorism. As John Negroponte, the US ambassador to the United Nations, explained in a letter to the President of the Security Council on 7 October 2001:

> The attacks on 11 September 2001 and the ongoing threat to the United States and its nationals posed by the al-Qaeda organization have been made possible by the decision of the Taliban regime to allow the parts of Afghanistan that it controls to be used by this organization as a base of operation. Despite every effort by the United States and the international community, the Taliban regime has refused to change its policy. From the territory of Afghanistan, the al-Qaeda organization continues to train and support agents of terror who attack innocent people throughout the world and target United States nationals and interests in the United States and abroad.

In this way, the United States broadened its claim of self-defence to necessitate action against the state of Afghanistan. Although still contentious, this claim was much less of a stretch from pre-existing international law than a claimed right to attack terrorists who simply happened to be within the territory of another country. Subsequent statements by the Taliban that endorsed the terrorist acts further raised the level of their alleged responsibility. For these reasons, the claim to be acting in self-defence against the country of Afghanistan – and the modification of customary international law that claim entailed – had a much better chance of securing the expressed or tacit support of other countries.

As the second part of its legal strategy, the United States worked hard to secure widespread support in advance of military action. The formation of a coalition, including the invocation of the collective self-defence provisions of the 1949 North Atlantic Treaty and the 1947 Inter-American Treaty of Reciprocal Assistance, helped smooth the path for the claim of self-defence. Both NATO and the Organization of American States formally deemed the events of 11 September 2001 an 'armed attack'. Similarly, UN Security Council resolutions adopted on 12 and 28 September 2001 were carefully worded to affirm the right of self-defence in customary international law, within the context of the terrorist attacks on New York and Washington, DC.

As a result of the law-making strategies adopted by the United States and heightened concern about terrorism worldwide, the right of self-defence now includes military responses against countries that willingly harbour or support terrorist groups, provided that the terrorists have already struck the responding state. And in accordance with a longstanding consensus – and Article 51 of the UN Charter – self-defence can be either individual or collective, so states that have been attacked by terrorists can call on other countries to assist them in their military response.

The long-term consequences of the US approach to self-defence and terrorism may be significant. Under the circumstances, had the Bush Administration relied on arguments of invitation, Security Council authorization, or even humanitarian intervention, few governments would have objected. But acting alone might have been made more difficult for the United States in future. Although previous attempts to establish a right of self-defence against terrorism had failed to attract widespread international support, the situation in the aftermath of 11 September 2001 was considerably more conducive. Having now seized the opportunity to establish self-defence as a basis for military action against terrorism, the United States, and other countries, will be able to invoke it again in circumstances which are less grave, and where the responsibility of the targeted state is less clear. This raises the question: where, then, are the limits of this new extension to the right of self-defence? The importance of the question is highlighted by the international debate over Israel's policy of 'targeted killing'.

Although it had been shaped by 11 September 2001, endorsed after action in Afghanistan, and honed in Iraq, the 'special relationship' between Britain and the United States was tested in 2004 as the governments of Tony Blair and George W. Bush disagreed publicly on a major issue of foreign policy. In mid-March, Hamas leader Sheikh Ahmad Yassin was killed by an Israeli missile as he left a mosque in his wheelchair. One month later his successor, Abdel-Aziz al-Rantissi, was killed in a similar attack. Jack Straw, the British Foreign Secretary, condemned the killings as 'unlawful'. In contrast, White House spokesman Scott McClellan asserted that 'Israel has the right to defend itself'. That the two principal partners in the 'war on terrorism' presented such starkly different conclusions on the legality of the Israeli action reflected their dissimilar perspectives on the Israeli-Palestinian situation, and on the relevant rules of international law.

From a European perspective, the Israeli missile strikes were 'extra-judicial killings' that violated fundamental principles of international human rights and humanitarian law. Global standards of due process require that suspected criminals be apprehended, prosecuted and convicted before being punished. Capital punishment is permitted, but death sentences can only be imposed by duly constituted courts. Yassin and Rantissi may well have incited and organized suicide bombings, but they should have been captured and prosecuted rather than simply killed.

Moreover, European governments consider the struggle between the Israelis and Palestinians to be primarily an 'occupation-gone-wrong', and view Israel, as an occupying power, as legally constrained by the rules set out in the Fourth Geneva Convention of 1949, the Convention relative to the Protection of Civilian Persons in Time of War. In support of this position, they point out that Jordan had administered the West Bank and East Jerusalem, and Egypt the Gaza Strip, prior to the seizure of these territories by Israel during the 1967 Six Day War. They also cite the encompassing language of Article 4(1): 'Persons protected by the Convention are those who, at a given moment and in any manner whatsoever, find themselves, in case of a conflict or occupation, in the hands of a Party to the conflict or Occupying Power of which they are not nationals.' Finally, European governments take the view that, at a minimum, Article 3 of the Geneva Convention applies to Israel, both as a treaty provision and as a codification of customary international law. The same Article 3 is found in all four of the 1949 Geneva Conventions; it is therefore referred to as 'Common Article 3'. Its first part is of relevance here:

> In the case of armed conflict not of an international character occurring in the territory of one of the High Contracting Parties, each Party to the conflict shall be bound to apply, as a minimum, the following provisions:
>
> 1. Persons taking no active part in the hostilities, including members of armed forces who have laid down their arms and those placed hors de combat by sickness, wounds, detention, or any other cause, shall in all circumstances be treated humanely, without any adverse distinction founded on race, colour, religion or faith, sex, birth or wealth, or any other similar criteria.
>
> To this end, the following acts are and shall remain prohibited at any time and in any place whatsoever with respect to the above-mentioned persons:
>
> (a) Violence to life and person, in particular murder of all kinds, mutilation, cruel treatment and torture;
> (b) Taking of hostages;
> (c) Outrages upon personal dignity, in particular humiliating and degrading treatment;
> (d) The passing of sentences and the carrying out of executions without previous judgment pronounced by a regularly constituted court, affording all the judicial guarantees which are recognized as indispensable by civilized peoples.

From the US government's perspective, Israel's actions were legal because the killings were aimed at preventing further terrorist attacks. The international law of self-defence – as opposed to that of human rights – provides the framework for this analysis. The policy of 'targeted killing' is seen as part of the global war on terrorism. In this respect, it is comparable to the 2001 invasion of Afghanistan, which the United States similarly justified as an act of self-defence.

The Israeli government, for its part, claims that the Fourth Geneva Convention is not applicable because the West Bank and Gaza Strip were not part of any state prior to being occupied by Israel. This view was firmly rejected by the International Court of Justice in a July 2004 advisory opinion on Israel's so-called 'security fence', though Israel has rejected the decision as biased. Israel also argues that, by the time suicide bombers reach its territory, it is too late to stop them; consequently, the only way to prevent attacks is to target pre-emptively the individuals responsible for planning them. In this sense, Yassin and Rantissi were actively engaged in hostilities. The Israeli position acquires a degree of credibility from the fact that both men publicly took credit for organizing suicide bombings in Israel, and threatened to conduct more.

As is so often the case, where one stands on this issue depends on where one sits. From the perspective of Jerusalem or Tel Aviv, suicide bombers pose a definite threat. Having lost more than 900 of their fellow citizens to Palestinian attacks since September 2000, Israelis believe they are at war. But how far might Prime Minister Ariel Sharon take the policy of targeted killing?

Following the Yassin and Rantissi killings, Sharon unilaterally 'released' himself from a pledge to President George W. Bush that Israel would not physically harm Yasser Arafat. At the time, the threat to the beleaguered Palestinian leader had to be taken seriously. And had he been openly harmed, the argument of self-defence would, almost certainly, again have been deployed.

The United States would have had difficulty opposing such an action, and not just because the Bush Administration repeatedly expressed support for Israel's prior targeted killings. Three days before Rantissi was killed, Bush endorsed Sharon's plan to retain the major Jewish settlements in the West Bank while pulling the Israeli army out of Gaza. Bush at the same time agreed to alter US policy concerning Palestinian refugees, accepting Israel's position that the refugees have no right to return to lands within Israel. With these two moves, the president abandoned any pretence that the United States could serve as an objective mediator in the Israel–Palestine conflict. Ariel Sharon now had the backing of the White House as he sought to impose – rather than negotiate – an outcome on Palestine. Yasser Arafat was written out of the script. Had he not died of other causes – and poison will never be ruled out – his 'targeted killing' might only have been a matter of time. His successor will live under the same threatening shadow.

Yet Arafat, unlike Yassin and Rantissi, was the democratically elected leader of a quasi-nation-state that has concluded treaties with Israel and holds observer status at the United Nations. He had not, during his time as leader of the Palestinian Authority, publicly claimed responsibility for or endorsed terrorist acts. Instead of hiding in the dangerous warren of Gaza City, Arafat was closely surrounded by Israeli forces in a readily identified location in Ramallah, and thus was easy to apprehend. His assassination, had it occurred, would have been a clear and egregious violation of international law, and properly criticized as such by the international community. His death in a Paris hospital was therefore the optimal outcome, at least for Ariel Sharon, and perhaps for the United States.

6

Pre-emptive Self-defence

On 7 June 1981, eight Israeli air force pilots conducted a bold and dangerous raid deep into hostile territory. Hugging the ground to avoid detection, they flew more than 600 miles before dropping their bombs on a nuclear reactor under construction at Osirak, on the outskirts of Baghdad. The reactor was badly damaged, Iraq's nuclear programme was severely impaired, and none of the attacking planes were lost. The pilots became national heroes. One of them, Ilan Ramon, was again a hero twenty-two years later when he became the first Israeli to journey into space on the ill-fated mission of the space shuttle *Columbia*.

Israel claimed pre-emptive self-defence for the strike on the basis that a nuclear-armed Iraq would constitute an unacceptable threat, especially given Saddam Hussein's overt hostility towards the Jewish state. Israel also claimed to have met the traditional requirement of proportionality, having bombed the construction site on a Sunday in order to lessen the risk to foreign workers. The Osirak reactor bombing thus involved an explicit claim to pre-emptive self-defence coupled with decisive military action. In the language of international law, both *opinio juris* and state practice were clearly present. But not only the state practice and *opinio juris* of the acting country matter in these situations; the responses of other governments are equally crucial.

Immediately after the attack on Osirak, the UN Security Council unanimously adopted a resolution condemning the Israeli action as illegal. This condemnation was even stronger because the United States joined in the vote rather than abstaining. That said, it is not entirely clear that all the members of the UN

Security Council voted for the condemnatory resolution because they were categorically opposed to pre-emptive self-defence. Because the Iraqi reactor was nowhere close to functioning at the time of the attack, some governments may have been more concerned about the fact that the traditional requirement of necessity had not been fulfilled. The important point, however, is that Israel expressly claimed the right to engage in pre-emptive military action against a possible, future threat and the international community resoundingly rejected the claim. In the British House of Commons, then Prime Minister Margaret Thatcher said that an 'armed attack in such circumstances cannot be justified. It represents a grave breach of international law.' Other governments were equally critical. Considered in its entirety, the state practice and *opinio juris* generated by the Israeli raid was against – rather than for – a right of pre-emptive self-defence.

This was not simply an issue of customary international law, since the first sentence of Article 51 of the UN Charter reads:

Nothing in the present Charter shall impair the inherent right of individual or collective self-defence if an armed attack occurs against a Member of the United Nations, until the Security Council has taken measures necessary to maintain international peace and security.

The rules of treaty interpretation, as codified in the 1969 Vienna Convention on the Law of Treaties, require that provisions be interpreted in accordance with the 'ordinary meaning of the terms'. When this approach is applied to Article 51, any pre-existing right of pre-emptive self-defence is apparently superseded by the requirement 'if an armed attack occurs'.

However, reference in Article 51 to the 'inherent' character of the right complicates the analysis by implicitly incorporating the pre-existing customary international law of self-defence into the treaty provision. Consequently, it is sometimes argued that pre-emptive action is justified if there is a 'necessity of self-defence, instant, overwhelming, leaving no choice of means, and no moment of deliberation'. These were the criteria set out by Daniel Webster after the 1837 *Caroline* incident, as discussed in Chapter 4. Until the adoption of the UN Charter in 1945, they were widely accepted as delimiting a narrow right of pre-emptive self-defence in customary international law. Today, with the Charter in force, these criteria can only succeed if Article 51 is ignored, re-read, or viewed as having been modified by subsequent state practice. Yet most of the state practice, including the widespread condemnation of the 1981 Israeli attack on the Osirak nuclear reactor, cuts the other way.

Indeed, since 1945, most governments have refrained from claiming pre-emptive self-defence. Israel, concerned not to be seen as an aggressor state, justified the strikes that initiated the 1967 Six Day War on the basis that Egypt's blocking of the Straits of Tiran constituted a prior act of aggression. The United States, concerned about establishing a precedent that other countries might employ, implausibly justified its 1962 blockade of Cuba as 'regional peace-keeping'. And in 1988, the United States similarly eschewed a claim of pre-emptive self-defence when it argued that the shooting down of an Iranian civilian Airbus by the USS *Vincennes*, although mistaken, had been in response to an ongoing attack by Iranian military helicopters and patrol boats. Even the most hawkish leaders baulked at a right of pre-emptive action during the Cold War, at a time when both the world's principal disputants possessed armadas of nuclear missile submarines designed to survive first strikes and ensure 'mutually assured destruction'.

Today, as seen from the White House, the situation looks quite different. Relations with Russia have improved dramatically, no other potential enemy has submarine-based nuclear missiles, and the first phase of a missile defence system has become operational (even though the technology is largely untested). When President George W. Bush announced an expansive new policy of pre-emptive military action on 1 June 2002, he clearly did not feel deterred by the prospect of Armageddon.

During a commencement speech at West Point, Bush addressed the threat of weapons of mass destruction (WMD) in association with international terrorism. The president advocated a degree of pre-emption that extended towards the preventive – or even precautionary – use of force: 'We must take the battle to the enemy, disrupt his plans, and confront the worst threats before they emerge.' Even if the threats are not imminent, 'if we wait for threats to fully materialize, we will have waited too long.' The new policy – now widely referred to as the 'Bush Doctrine' – made no attempt to satisfy the *Caroline* criteria. There was no suggestion of waiting for a 'necessity of self-defence' that was 'instant, over-whelming, leaving no choice of means, and no moment of deliberation'. The new policy is questionable on several levels.

Is unilateral military action the best way to deal with WMD? Weapons of mass destruction are hardly a new problem. The first treaty on poison gas dates back to 1899. For decades the United Nations has led efforts to control the development and spread of such weapons while, ironically, the United States has dragged its feet. The Bush Administration, shortly after coming to power, refused to ratify enforcement protocols to the Chemical and Biological Weapons Conventions. The Bush Administration pressured 139 countries into dismissing José Bustani, the highly regarded director-general of the Organization for the Prohibition of Chemical Weapons, in the middle of his term; it is now pushing for the removal of Mohamed ElBaradei, the head of the International Atomic Energy Agency. The Bush Administration, in violation of its obligations under the Nuclear Non-Proliferation Treaty, has accelerated efforts to develop battlefield nuclear weapons designed to penetrate deep bunkers and destroy dangerous chemicals and pathogens. And the Bush Administration actively opposes the International Criminal Court, which could prosecute individuals for using WMD. All of this could reasonably lead one to question whether George W. Bush has really provided leadership on the weapons of mass destruction issue.

A broad right of pre-emptive self-defence would also introduce dangerous uncertainties into international relations. Who would decide that a potential threat justifies pre-emptive action? How does one protect against opportunistic military interventions justified under the guise of pre-emptive self-defence? Do we wish to accord the same extended right to India, Pakistan or Israel – all nuclear powers with a history of engaging in cross-border interventions – as the equal applicability of customary international law would require us to do? Could the development of such a right prompt potential targets into striking first, using rather than losing their biological, chemical and nuclear weapons? Governments are intensely aware of the potentially dangerous consequences of the Bush Doctrine and most have been cautious about giving it their support.

Their concerns are heightened by the fact that the UN Charter already provides an answer to these questions: in the absence of an attack, only the UN Security Council can act. Provided with clear evidence of an imminent biological, chemical or nuclear attack, there is little doubt that the Security Council would act, since the effects of weapons of mass destruction are unlikely to be confined within a discrete geographical area. In recent years, the Security Council has repeatedly authorized military action in situations where there has been no direct or immediate threat to its fifteen members: in Iraq, Somalia, Bosnia-Herzegovina, Haiti and elsewhere. After the terrorist attacks of 11 September 2001, it took the Council only one day to affirm the right of the United States to engage in self-defence in that instance.

Only countries with no reason to fear countervailing military forces can contemplate a world without the combined protections of the UN Charter and the customary law of the *Caroline* incident. President Bush feels able to claim a broad right of pre-emptive action because other states do not have the capacity to retaliate against the United States. What the Bush Administration apparently fails to realize is that its actions might well provide incentives – perversely based on self-defence – for others to acquire the very weapons that the United States purports to abhor.

The staff lawyers and diplomats in the US State Department were undoubtedly aware of the potentially negative consequences of the President's words at West Point; words intended to convey a policy decision that had, in all likelihood, been made with little consideration of international law. The State Department lawyers had the task of justifying the new policy in legal terms. They would have soon realized that, as expressed, the new policy was not only ill-advised and unprecedented, but had little chance of becoming customary international law. Simply put, most countries do not stand to benefit from an extended right of pre-emptive self-defence because it would give all states – including every state's potential enemies – an almost unlimited discretion to use force. The absence of widely reciprocal benefits is usually fatal to the development of customary international law, which, as we have seen, requires not only the advancement of a claim but also widespread support or acquiescence.

Accordingly, the Bush Doctrine was reformulated to make it more acceptable to other countries, and thereby more effective in promoting legal change. The National Security Strategy of the United States, released on 20 September 2002, explicitly adopted – and then sought to extend – the criteria for self-defence articulated by Daniel Webster following the *Caroline* incident:

> For centuries, international law recognized that nations need not suffer an attack before they can lawfully take action to defend themselves against forces that present an imminent danger of attack. Legal scholars and international jurists often conditioned the legitimacy of preemption on the existence of an imminent threat – most often a visible mobilization of armies, navies, and air forces preparing to attack.
>
> We must adapt the concept of imminent threat to the capabilities and objectives of today's adversaries.

The National Security Strategy made no mention of the UN Charter, implicitly asserting by omission that the pre-1945 customary right of self-defence remained the applicable law. By glossing over the normally contentious issue of the relationship between the *Caroline* criteria and Article 51, the document strategically sought to establish a new baseline for the discussion of self-defence. Only then did it go further, asserting that the criterion of imminence now extends beyond threats which are 'instant, overwhelming, leaving no choice of means, and no moment of deliberation' to include more distant and uncertain challenges.

This claim was made within a context that at least suggested the need for legal change. Few would contest that terrorism and WMD are serious problems. As significantly, other governments were not asked to agree on an actual change to the rule. Instead, all that was proposed in the National Security Strategy was an adaptation of how the (supposed) existing rule is applied in practice. The claim thus appears patently reasonable and, as such, well suited to generate widespread support and acquiescence. Such support and acquiescence, once combined with military action justified on the basis of the claim, could quickly generate new customary international law.

Yet the reformulated doctrine of pre-emptive self-defence is not as innocuous as it first appears. By adopting and stretching the pre-1945 criterion of imminence, the approach advocated in the National Security Strategy could introduce much more ambiguity into the law. This ambiguity could, in turn, allow power and influence to play a greater role in the application of the law. In future, whether the criterion of imminence is fulfilled would depend in large part on the factual circumstances – as assessed by individual states and groups of states. And the ability of the powerful to influence these assessments could be considerable, given the various forms of political, economic and military pressure that can be brought to bear in international affairs. In addition, powerful countries sometimes have special knowledge based on secret intelligence, or at least claim such knowledge in an attempt to augment their influence, as occurred in the lead-up to the 2003 Iraq War. As a result, the criterion of imminence would more likely be regarded as fulfilled when the United States wished to act militarily than when other countries wished to do the same. The law on self-defence would remain generally applicable – available as a diplomatic tool to be deployed against weak states – while the most powerful of countries would have more freedom to act as they chose.

Fortunately, the US government does not have a monopoly on good international lawyers. A few regional powers, such as India, Israel and Russia, did respond favourably to the claim set out in the National Security Strategy, as did Australian Prime Minister John Howard, who suggested that the UN Charter be amended to allow for a right of unilateral pre-emptive action. But Howard's comments sparked angry protests from other Southeast Asian states – protests which could themselves constitute state practice and evidence of *opinio juris* against a right of pre-emptive self-defence. Other countries, including France, Germany and Mexico, expressed concern in more moderate terms, while Japan voiced support for a right of pre-emptive self-defence but was careful to confine its claim to the *Caroline* criteria.

As the Iraq crisis escalated, this at-best mixed reaction contributed to bringing the United States to the UN Security Council where, on 8 November 2002, it obtained Resolution 1441. As was explained in Chapter 3, the resolution did not expressly authorize the use of force against Iraq but did provide some support for an argument that a previous authorization, accorded in 1990, had been revived as a result of Iraq's 'material breaches' of the 1991 ceasefire resolution. The Bush Administration relied on both this argument and the pre-emptive self-defence claim to justify the 2003 Iraq War, while its two principal allies, Britain and Australia, relied solely on the Security Council resolutions. The advancement of two distinct arguments, with the latter receiving broader support, reduced any effect that the claim to an extended right of pre-emptive self-defence might have had on customary international law.

Following the war, widespread opposition to the Bush Doctrine was evident in the opening speeches of the 58th session of the UN General Assembly in September 2003. Hidipo Hamutenya, the Foreign Minister of Namibia, observed that 'the central theme, that runs through nearly all the speeches at this Session, is the call for a return to multilateral dialogue, persuasion and collective action, as the only appropriate approach to resolving many conflicts facing the international community'.

In light of this and other negative reactions, it is difficult to argue that the claim to an extended right of pre-emptive self-defence has obtained the widespread support necessary to change customary international law or, perhaps, Article 51 of the UN Charter. Yet the claim continues to be made. In a television interview on 7 February 2004, President Bush went so far as to say: 'I believe it is essential – that when we see a threat, we deal with those threats before they become imminent. It's too late if they become imminent. It's too late in this new kind of war.'

In December 2004, the UN Secretary General's High Level Panel on Threats, Challenges and Change, a group of sixteen former prime ministers, foreign ministers and ambassadors (including Brent Scowcroft, who served as National Security Adviser to President George H. W. Bush), presented its highly authoritative response to the US president's claim:

> The short answer is that if there are good arguments for preventive military action, with good evidence to support them, they should be put to the Security Council, which can authorize such action if it chooses to. If it does not so choose, there will be, by definition, time to pursue other strategies, including persuasion, negotiation, deterrence and containment – and to visit again the military option.
>
> For those impatient with such a response, the answer must be that, in a world full of perceived potential threats, the risk to the global order and the norm of non-intervention on which it continues to be based is simply too great for the legality of

unilateral preventive action, as distinct from collectively endorsed action, to be accepted. Allowing one to so act is to allow all.

The report was a stinging rebuke to the Bush Administration, and intended to be understood as such. The goal was not to change the president's mind (it will not), but to rally and reinforce international opposition to his dangerously destabilizing doctrine of pre-emptive war.

Part Three

Humanitarian Intervention

7

Pro-Democratic Intervention

United Nations Security Council authorization and the right of self-defence are written exceptions to the prohibition on the use of force and expressly set out in the UN Charter. Two further, unwritten exceptions may have developed in recent decades: a right to intervene militarily to promote or restore democracy, and a right to intervene to prevent serious human rights abuses or violations of international humanitarian law such as genocide, mass expulsion or systematic rape. This chapter considers 'pro-democratic intervention'. Chapter 8 examines 'humanitarian intervention'.

One year after the 2003 Iraq War, President George W. Bush and Prime Minister Tony Blair began speaking passionately about the importance of bringing 'democracy and freedom' to Iraq and the Middle East. The implication was obvious: the promotion of democracy was an after-the-fact justification for the war. Yet the democracy argument was not invoked until Iraq's alleged weapons of mass destruction – the principal justification for the war both under Resolution 1441 and the Bush Doctrine of pre-emptive self-defence – proved more elusive than expected. Credible legal justifications cannot be made retroactively. The failure to advance the democracy argument at the time of the invasion of Iraq suggests, among other things, an absence of belief (*opinio juris*) in the legality of the claim.

There are no credible precedents for the claim of pro-democratic intervention. In the absence of precedents, there is no supporting state practice or *opinio juris* and, therefore, no possible rule of customary international law. The UN Security Council could authorize an intervention for the purposes of supporting or restoring democracy, as it arguably did in Haiti in 1994, but individual countries or groups of countries cannot legally take such action on their own. Even the two possible precedents cited by some academics – the invasions of Grenada (1983) and Panama (1989) – do not provide assistance here. Closer scrutiny of these interventions reveals that, if anything, they reinforce the contrary rule: that the use of force to promote democracy is prohibited under customary international law unless expressly authorized by the Security Council.

Four hundred US marines and 1,500 paratroopers landed on the Caribbean island nation of Grenada on 25 October 1983, together with 300 soldiers from neighbouring Caribbean countries. The invasion came in response to a violent *coup d'état* by radical Marxist opponents of the democratically elected government of Maurice Bishop. It took just three days for the invading soldiers to depose the newly self-appointed Revolutionary Military Council. The US troops were home within eight weeks. Casualties numbered just over 100: 18 Americans, some 45 Grenadines (including 21 civilians killed in the accidental bombing of a hospital) and 34 Cuban soldiers (who were supporting the Marxists).

The Reagan Administration offered several justifications for the invasion. First, the United States cited an invitation from the Governor-General of Grenada received the day before the invasion was launched. However, evidence of the actual invitation is elusive. *The Economist*, which strongly supported the invasion, reported that the 'request was almost certainly a fabrication concocted between the OECS [Organization of Eastern Caribbean States] and Washington to calm the post-invasion diplomatic storm'. Moreover, the invasion was already in an advanced stage of implementation by the time the request would have been received. Although the timing of the request does not touch on the legality of the invasion, it does indicate that the invitation was not considered decisive by the United States.

Second, the United States cited a request to intervene from the OECS and claimed that the request was of legal import under Article 52 of the UN Charter. However, Article 52 deals solely with the 'pacific settlement of local disputes'. Forceful actions by regional organizations are dealt with under Article 53, where it is made clear that 'no enforcement action shall be taken under regional arrangements or by regional agencies without the authorization of the Security Council'. Authorization had not been provided with regard to Grenada.

Finally, the United States advanced a claim of self-defence for the protection of nationals, a specific rule discussed in Chapter 4. Yet the facts supporting the claim have been disputed. The United States asserted that Grenadine officials had refused to allow its citizens to leave the island, while Canada claimed to have flown a chartered plane to and from Grenada on the day of the invasion. In any event, David Robinson, the Legal Adviser at the US State Department at the time, subsequently admitted that the scale of the operation exceeded the limits of this 'well-established, narrowly drawn ground for the use of force'.

The United States never claimed that it was intervening in Grenada to restore democracy. In fact, David Robinson went so far as to stress the grounds on which it did *not* rely: an expanded view of self-defence, 'new interpretations' of Article 2(4) of the UN Charter, or 'a broad doctrine of "humanitarian intervention"'. The same is true of the Caribbean states involved, who claimed that the action was 'to help stabilize the country', 'restore law and order' and, above all, 'block the Russians and the Cubans'. Even if the United States and its allies had invoked the restoration of democracy to justify the intervention, the most relevant state practice and evidence of *opinio juris* would be the negative reactions of other governments. A UN Security Council resolution that would have condemned the invasion was vetoed by the United States. The General Assembly, free of such constraints, 'deeply deplored' the US-led action as a flagrant violation of international law. Rather than providing support for a right of pro-democratic intervention, the invasion of Grenada helped strengthen the rule against such actions.

On 20 December 1989, the United States deployed 26,000 troops to overthrow the government of Panama and capture its head of state, General Manuel Noriega. President George H. W. Bush justified the action on four grounds: 'to safeguard the lives of Americans, to defend democracy in Panama, to combat drug trafficking, and to protect the integrity of the Panama Canal Treaty'. Having captured Noriega, the United States recognized the 'rightful leadership' of the likely victors of elections that had been held earlier that year. Diplomatic relations would resume immediately, steps would be taken to lift the economic sanctions imposed against the Noriega regime, and US forces would be withdrawn 'as quickly as possible'. Apparently oblivious to the irony, Bush added that he would 'continue to seek solutions to the problems of this region through dialogue and multilateral diplomacy'. Analysis of the legal basis for the action – optimistically codenamed 'Just Cause' – is made difficult by the conflation of policy and legal reasoning in such statements.

Of the four grounds outlined above, the protection of nationals most closely resembled a legal argument. During the UN Security Council debate on the matter, the US ambassador stated: 'I am not here today to claim a right on behalf of the United States to enforce the will of history by intervening in favour of democracy where we are not welcomed. We are supporters of democracy but not the gendarmes of democracy, not in this hemisphere or anywhere else...We acted in Panama for legitimate reasons of self-defence and to protect the integrity of the Canal Treaties.'

While the right of self-defence in protection of nationals was the primary legal justification advanced by Washington, the defence of democracy claim garnered the most support from academics. Professor Anthony D'Amato of Northwestern University described US actions in Panama (and previously Grenada) as 'milestones along the path to a new nonstatist conception of international law'. Professor Michael Reisman of Yale University heralded a new era in which 'the people, not governments, are sovereign'. In a remarkably isolationist conception of customary international law, each scholar ignored – or at least discounted as irrelevant – the broad condemnation of the Panama intervention by the international community. A strongly condemnatory draft UN Security Council resolution was vetoed by the United States and Britain, while similar resolutions were adopted by the General Assembly – where all UN members are represented – and the Organization of American States.

The US government invoked democracy to support the invasion of Panama in two ways: as the exercise of a right to act unilaterally to promote democracy in other countries, and as the provision of assistance to a democratically elected head of state, Guillermo Endara, who had ostensibly consented to the action. But the United States never claimed that Endara had requested the invasion. Although Bush stated that Endara 'welcomed the assistance' of the United States and there was some reference to him having been 'consulted', Endara was not informed of the invasion until the troops were in the air. Journalist Bob Woodward reported that Bush had decided this was the point of no return and that, if Endara refused to 'play ball', Secretary of Defense Dick Cheney and General Colin Powell – who were overseeing the operation – were to check with Bush personally. Endara was sworn in as President of Panama at Fort Clayton, a US military base in the US-controlled Canal Zone, less than an hour before the invasion began.

There is, in fact, evidence that Endara was not entirely pleased with the operation, having later described it as a 'kick in the head'. In any event, most Latin American countries withdrew their ambassadors from Panama after the invasion and refused to recognize the Endara government, stating that diplomatic relations would be normalized only when the number of US troops in the country returned to pre-invasion levels and a plebiscite demonstrated popular support for the new regime. The Permanent

Council of the Organization of American States initially refused to accept the credentials of the ambassador dispatched by Endara. Noriega's ambassador remained at the organization's headquarters in Washington and participated in the vote that criticized the invasion. Some months passed before most countries recognized Panama's new government. This widespread reluctance to recognize the Endara government, coupled with strong objections from many states in the UN Security Council, the condemnatory resolution adopted by the UN General Assembly, and the fact that the restoration of democracy was only one of four justifications advanced by the United States, are further evidence that pro-democratic intervention remains prohibited under international law. George Bush and Tony Blair can talk all they want about the need to bring 'democracy and freedom' to the Middle East, but they cannot, by themselves, create a new right to military action.

The UN Charter's prohibition on the use of force also bars the provision of forceful assistance to opposition groups, even those seeking to bring democracy to their country. In 1970, the UN General Assembly adopted a 'Friendly Relations Resolution' that encapsulated the rule:

> Every State has the duty to refrain from organizing, instigating, assisting or participating in acts of civil strife or terrorist acts in another State or acquiescing in organized activities within its territory directed towards the commission of such acts, when the acts referred to in the present paragraph involve a threat or use of force.

The International Court of Justice reaffirmed the rule in 1986, in the *Nicaragua Case*, where the government of Nicaragua successfully sued Washington for using force, and particularly for training and equipping the Contras, the right-wing opposition forces operating out of neighbouring Honduras. The only exception to the rule – and it remains controversial – concerns support for national liberation movements seeking to expel colonial powers. Financial assistance to opposition groups is likewise permitted because no force is used.

If pro-democratic intervention and forceful assistance to opposition groups are both prohibited, what then of interventions, not authorized by the UN Security Council, that are aimed at preventing governments from committing mass atrocities against their own citizens? This issue – unilateral humanitarian intervention – is the subject of the next chapter.

8

Unilateral Humanitarian Intervention

The prohibition on the use of force has increasingly been challenged by scholars, politicians and commentators who believe that national governments that systematically murder, rape or expel their own citizens should not be shielded against military intervention. Convinced that the UN Security Council cannot be relied upon to address these problems, and that the United Nations – rather than its member states – is somehow to blame, they argue for a right of 'unilateral humanitarian intervention', that is, a right to intervene for humanitarian purposes without the authorization of the Security Council.

Advocates of such a right cite a handful of possible precedents, including India's intervention in East Pakistan (1971), Vietnam's intervention in Cambodia (1978), Tanzania's intervention in Uganda (1979) and the intervention in Northern Iraq (1991) by Britain, France, Italy, the Netherlands and the United States. A brief examination of these four instances reveals that none of the intervening countries, apart from Britain in 1991, advanced an argument of humanitarian intervention. Even then, Britain quickly abandoned its claim in favour of arguing that it had the implied authorization of the UN Security Council, as discussed in Chapter 3. Overall, this near absence of *opinio juris* deprived the state practice of any capacity to change international law to allow a right of unilateral humanitarian intervention.

The Kosovo War (1999) is frequently cited as having changed this calculus in favour of a new rule, though in the end only two NATO countries claimed a legal right to humanitarian interven-

tion. And, as was the case when India invaded East Pakistan in
1971, most countries publicly opposed the war.

A largely Muslim country comprising East and West Pakistan was
created as a result of the decolonization and partition of India in
1947. Although Bengali-speaking East Pakistan was separated
from Urdu-speaking West Pakistan by more than 1,000 miles of
Indian territory, the western province dominated political,
economic and military affairs. In 1970, the Awami League, a political party that advocated autonomy for East Pakistan, won the
majority of seats – and all but two of East Pakistan's seats – in the
Pakistani National Assembly. Pakistan's military president,
General Yahya Khan, responded by refusing to convene the
Assembly. Widespread demonstrations then broke out, and Khan
invoked martial law. In March 1971, the leader of the Awami
League, Sheikh Mujibur Rahman, was arrested and taken to West
Pakistan. On 26 March, his party issued a 'Declaration of
Emancipation'. General Khan immediately sent the Pakistani
army into Dacca.

At least one million people were killed in the following nine
months, many of them children and most of them Hindu. The
ethnic dimension of the conflict led the International Commission
of Jurists, a widely respected non-governmental organization, to
identify the campaign of violence as an apparent genocide. Awami
League members were arrested, tortured and killed, as were countless community leaders. Women were systematically raped,
villages looted and destroyed, and up to ten million people fled
across the border into India.

The vast number of refugees caused massive social, economic
and administrative problems for India and relations between New
Delhi and Islamabad declined sharply. India provided refuge and
air support for the Mukti Bahini, an armed Bengali liberation
movement, and border incidents multiplied. War broke out on 3
December 1971 when Pakistan bombed ten Indian military
airfields. Within days, India had occupied most of East Pakistan

and recognized the province as the sovereign and independent country of Bangladesh. The Pakistani Army surrendered after just twelve days of fighting and Sheikh Mujibur returned to Dacca to become prime minister. Three years later, the new country was admitted to the United Nations.

Professor Fernando Tesón of Florida State University has described the Indian action as 'an almost perfect example' of humanitarian intervention. The use of force did stop a horrific campaign of repression. Yet the India government advanced a very different legal claim. Although humanitarian grounds figured prominently in the political justifications that were advanced initially, this rhetoric was soon replaced by a legal argument of self-defence. As India's representative on the UN Security Council explained, 'We decided to silence their guns, to save our civilians.'

Even the use of humanitarian crisis as political justification was opposed strongly by other countries. During the UN Security Council debate following the intervention, the US representative said: 'The fact that the use of force in East Pakistan in March can be characterized as a tragic mistake does not, however, justify the actions of India in intervening militarily and placing in jeopardy the territorial integrity and political independence of its neighbour Pakistan.' Even Sweden, a notably progressive country on international human rights issues, emphasized that 'the Charter of the United Nations forbids the use of force except in self-defence. No other purpose can justify the use of military force by States.' A Security Council resolution calling for a ceasefire and the immediate withdrawal of Indian troops from the country was vetoed by the Soviet Union, which at the time was a close ally of India. The UN General Assembly adopted essentially the same resolution in a 104–11 vote, with ten abstentions. Most importantly, not one country endorsed India's humanitarian intervention claim, so no *opinio juris* was expressed in its favour.

In the period between 1975 and 1978, the Khmer Rouge government of Cambodia (Kampuchea) murdered hundreds of thousands of its own citizens and implemented policies that killed millions more through starvation and disease. Under the leadership of General Pol Pot, the Khmer Rouge also launched a series of cross-border attacks on Vietnam. Vietnam responded by invading Cambodia on 25 December 1978. Fighting alongside Cambodian opposition forces, Vietnamese troops quickly established control over most of the country, capturing Phnom Penh on 7 January 1979.

Vietnam claimed that it was acting solely to defend itself against Cambodian aggression, and that the overthrow of Pol Pot's regime was the result of an internal uprising. The self-defence argument was widely rejected by other countries, apart from Vietnam's closest allies: the Soviet Union and its satellite states. However, since the invasion ended the humanitarian crisis, and since the suffering involved had been of such huge dimension, most governments felt it necessary to go further and address the possibility that stopping the atrocities might somehow have legitimized the use of military force. For example, the French representative to the UN Security Council said:

> The notion that because a regime is detestable foreign intervention is justified and forcible overthrow is legitimate is extremely dangerous. That could ultimately jeopardize the very maintenance of international law and order and make the continued existence of various regimes dependent on the judgement of their neighbours.

Similar emphatic statements were made by Australia, Britain, France, Indonesia, Malaysia, Nigeria, Norway, the Philippines, Portugal, Singapore and Yugoslavia. Even Bangladesh, the beneficiary of India's 1971 invasion of East Pakistan, reaffirmed the principle of non-intervention in domestic affairs. A resolution to the same effect was introduced in the Security Council by seven of its developing country members. The document also called on all foreign forces – Vietnamese forces – to withdraw. Thirteen countries voted in favour of the resolution, and only two – the Soviet Union and Czechoslovakia – voted against it, with the Soviet vote acting as a veto.

The UN General Assembly was equally unsupportive of what Vietnam had done. In September 1979 it rejected a demand for accreditation from the new, Vietnamese-sponsored government in Phnom Penh and instead accepted the credentials of a Khmer Rouge delegation. General Pol Pot's regime, confined to a remote area near the border with Thailand, represented Cambodia in the General Assembly for nine more years. In November 1979, the General Assembly voted 91–21, with 29 abstentions, in favour of a resolution that demanded the immediate withdrawal of all foreign forces and an end to interference in the domestic affairs of Southeast Asian states.

A handful of countries did support the Vietnamese action on humanitarian grounds. For example, the East German representative to the UN General Assembly asserted that 'the assistance of Vietnam in the struggle for a new Kampuchea was primarily a humanitarian matter. It rescued the Kampuchean people from total destruction.' Such expressions of support, however, were not only in the minority, but came from countries that had less-than-stellar human rights records. Democratic, human rights-respecting countries condemned unanimously both the Vietnamese intervention and the atrocities committed by Pol Pot's regime. As the Norwegian representative to the United Nations explained:

> The Norwegian Government and public opinion in Norway have expressed strong objections to the serious violations of human rights committed by the Pol Pot Government. However, the domestic policies of that Government cannot – we repeat, cannot – justify the actions of Vietnam over the last days and weeks. The Norwegian Government firmly rejects the threat or use of force against the territorial integrity or political independence of any State.

The 1978 Vietnamese invasion of Cambodia provides no support for a right of unilateral humanitarian intervention in international law. During the Cold War, geopolitical competition between the United States and the Soviet Union precluded any new exception to the prohibition of the use of force in international affairs.

Idi Amin served as president of Uganda for eight bloodstained years. He and his henchmen murdered some 300,000 of their fellow citizens and countless more were tortured, raped or otherwise brutalized. Although many countries condemned the Ugandan regime for these human rights violations, no significant action was taken until 1978 when Amin sent troops into neighbouring Tanzania and declared that he was annexing the northwest corner of that country. Julius Nyerere, the President of Tanzania and one of Africa's most respected heads of state, responded that the purported annexation was 'tantamount to an act of war'. Nyerere ordered his troops to push Amin's forces back into Uganda. The Ugandan dictator made a plea for reinforcements and Libya's Colonel Muammar Qaddafi obliged, sending 2,500 troops. In March 1979, Tanzania launched a full-fledged counter-attack. With the help of Ugandan rebels, the Tanzanian troops soon overwhelmed the Ugandan army, gained control of the country and installed Yusufu Lule as president. Amin fled into exile, first to Libya and later to Saudi Arabia, where he lived in luxury until his death in August 2003.

Despite Amin's atrocious human rights record, Tanzania never sought to justify its intervention on humanitarian grounds, relying instead on a claim of self-defence. As Nyerere explained:

> The war between Tanzania and Idi Amin's regime in Uganda was caused by the Ugandan Army's aggression against Tanzania and Idi Amin's claim to have annexed part of Tanzania. There was no other cause for it.

Tanzania also asserted, much as Vietnam had done eight years earlier, that a domestic uprising had led to the overthrow of the opposing government. In this instance, most countries accepted the self-defence claim, some of them – including Angola, Botswana, Mozambique and Zambia – expressly, but most tacitly. When Amin asked that the UN Security Council meet to discuss the situation, the request fell on deaf ears. The UN General Assembly accredited the new Ugandan government less than six months after Amin was ousted from power. Tanzanian forces were out of the country within two years.

A few academic international lawyers have invoked Tanzania's actions as a precedent for a right of unilateral humanitarian intervention. The atrocities committed by the Amin dictatorship could have provided a strong factual basis, but only if Tanzania had chosen to make the claim. Even then, the weight of the precedent would depend on the reaction of other countries. But Tanzania never claimed a humanitarian motivation, let alone a right to intervene for humanitarian purposes. This absence of *opinio juris* on the part of the acting power renders the intervention in Uganda irrelevant to legal discussions concerning unilateral humanitarian intervention, except as a reflection of the general awareness that no such right could plausibly be claimed.

Some of the geopolitical constraints on a possible right of unilateral humanitarian intervention changed after the collapse of the Soviet Union and the end of the Cold War, though widespread support for a change in international law has yet to appear.

During the 1991 Gulf War, the United States encouraged the Kurds of northern Iraq and the Shiites of southern Iraq to rebel against Saddam Hussein's regime. Yet Resolution 687, adopted by the UN Security Council to secure and regulate the ceasefire between Iraq and the coalition forces, did nothing to protect the Kurds and Shiites from the violent retribution that followed. As news of the horrors reached Western capitals and hundreds of thousands of desperate refugees appeared on television screens, the Security Council begrudgingly passed Resolution 688. This resolution identified the situation as a threat to international peace and security, called on the Iraqi government to end the repression and demanded access to northern Iraq for international humanitarian organizations. On this basis, in April 1991, American, British, Dutch, French and Italian forces were deployed in northern Iraq as part of 'Operation Provide Comfort', establishing so-called 'safe havens' to protect Kurdish civilians.

Resolution 688 did not expressly authorize the use of force against Iraq. The intervening countries weakly suggested that the Security Council's determination of a threat to international peace and security constituted implicit authority for their actions. One country – the United Kingdom – used the occasion to advance a doctrine of unilateral humanitarian intervention when the British Foreign and Commonwealth Office said:

> We believe that international intervention without the invitation of the country concerned can be justified in cases of extreme humanitarian need. This is why we were prepared to commit British forces to *Operation Haven*, mounted by the coalition in response to the refugee crisis involving the Iraqi Kurds.

The Foreign Office proceeded to suggest that the doctrine should be limited to situations where: 1) there is a compelling and urgent situation of extreme humanitarian distress; 2) the state targeted by the intervention is unable or unwilling to act; 3) there is no practical alternative; and 4) the intervention is limited in time and scope. Although the claim was unprecedented among governments, it was also deliberately restrained. The British government never specifically claimed a 'legal' right, speaking instead of 'justification', which could refer to moral, political or legal grounds. And the United Kingdom did not advance the claim in the United Nations, probably out of concern that it would be badly received.

Even if there were considerable state practice and *opinio juris* in favour of a right of unilateral humanitarian intervention, the international law on this issue might remain unchanged. Since clear treaty provisions prevail over customary international law, a customary rule allowing intervention would be insufficient to override Article 2(4) of the UN Charter. Nor could deficiencies in the United Nations system enable countries to fall back on a customary rule allowing intervention on humanitarian grounds. When, in the 1949 *Corfu Channel Case*, Britain sought to justify an intervention in Albanian territorial waters on the basis that no one else was prepared to deal with the threat of mines laid in an international strait, the International Court of Justice ruled:

> The Court cannot accept this line of defence. The Court can only regard the alleged right of intervention as the manifestation of a policy of force, such as has, in the past, given rise to the most serious abuses and such as cannot, whatever be the present defects in international organization, find a place in international law.

Accordingly, in light of Article 2(4) of the UN Charter, any right of unilateral humanitarian intervention could have effect only if it achieved the status of *jus cogens*, a peremptory rule that overrides conflicting treaty provisions. This clearly had not occurred before 1999, but what then of the Kosovo War? Did the state practice and *opinio juris* associated with that intervention constitute the broad consensus necessary to generate a new customary rule with the capacity to override the UN Charter?

Albanian and Slavic peoples have coexisted in Kosovo since the eighth century. Initially part of the Serbian Empire, Kosovo became part of the Ottoman Empire in 1389. Serbia regained control in 1913 and in 1946 Kosovo became part of the Federal Republic of Yugoslavia. When Slobodan Milošević became president of Yugoslavia in 1989, one of his first acts was to strip Kosovo of its status as an autonomous province. Following the break-up of Yugoslavia in the early 1990s, and facing increasingly frequent attacks on Serb targets by an ethnic Albanian guerrilla movement, the Kosovo Liberation Army (KLA), President Milošević initiated a brutal crackdown that provided all the indications of a genocide in the making. The United States and its European allies, embarrassed by their failure to stop the earlier atrocities in Bosnia-Herzegovina, warned that such acts would not be tolerated. The UN Security Council twice deemed the situation a threat to 'international peace and security' before Milošević – now being threatened with war by NATO (a regional *defence* alliance) – agreed to internationally brokered negotiations with the KLA at Rambouillet, France. The negotiations came close to securing a peace agreement, until Milošević baulked at a patently unreasonable provision that would have granted NATO forces unrestricted access to all Yugoslav territory, not just in Kosovo.

Although the numbers of Kosovo-Albanians killed, raped or expelled up to this point were low, the credibility of NATO's threats was at issue. On 24 March 1999, the United States and a number of other NATO countries inaugurated a long campaign of air strikes against Serbian forces in Kosovo and government targets in Serbia and Montenegro. They did so without attempting, in the couple of months before the attack, to discuss the matter in the UN Security Council. A Security Council resolution condemning the attack was quickly proposed by Russia, but defeated, in large part because the five NATO countries then on the Council voted against it.

In the end, only two NATO countries – initially the United Kingdom and later Belgium – sought to justify the Kosovo War on the basis of a legal right to unilateral humanitarian intervention. NATO Secretary General Javier Solana confined himself to saying, 'We must halt the violence and bring an end to the humanitarian catastrophe now unfolding.' There was thus a remarkable absence of *opinio juris* to accompany the state practice involved in the intervention. Russia, China and India spoke out strongly against the war, as did Namibia (which had voted in the Security Council to condemn the bombings), Belarus, Ukraine, Iran, Thailand, Indonesia and South Africa. Following the intervention, the 133 developing countries of the 'Group of 77' twice adopted declarations unequivocally affirming that unilateral humanitarian intervention was illegal under international law.

Shortly after the war ended, the UN Security Council adopted Resolution 1244, which gave the United Nations a central role in Kosovo's reconstruction. Although the resolution was carefully worded to preclude any argument that it retroactively authorized the war, some academics have argued that it did so. Similar arguments have been made about the defeat of the Russian-proposed resolution condemning the intervention. These arguments ignore the fact that the UN Charter requires a positive rather than negative authorization, and the possibility that a less angrily worded draft might have attracted more support.

The Kosovo War was neither consistent with international law nor effective in changing the law in favour of a right of unilateral humanitarian intervention. As the International Court of Justice indicated in the 1986 *Nicaragua Case*, international rules usually continue in force despite the occasional violation:

> It is not to be expected that in the practice of States the application of the rules in question should have been perfect, in the sense that States should have refrained, with complete consistency, from the use of force or from intervention in each other's internal affairs. ... In order to deduce the existence of customary rules, the Court deems it sufficient that the conduct of States should, in general, be consistent with such rules, and that instances of State conduct inconsistent with a given rule should generally be treated as breaches of that rule, not as indications of the recognition of a new rule.

Much more state practice and *opinio juris* would be needed before a right of unilateral humanitarian intervention, as an exception to the well-established prohibition of the use of force, could reasonably be considered to have acquired legal force. Even then, any new rule of customary international law would not – unless it somehow achieved *jus cogens* status – override Article 2(4) of the UN Charter. For these reasons, the significance of humanitarian concerns to the international law on the recourse to force remains at the level of political will – and moral and political justification, including what is now called the 'responsibility to protect'.

9

Responsibility to Protect

Following the 1999 Kosovo War, the British Foreign Office submitted a proposal to the United Nations for a carefully defined, limited right of unilateral (i.e. not Security Council authorized) humanitarian intervention – one that 1) would only be available as a last resort; 2) addressed an overwhelming humanitarian catastrophe which the territorial government was unable or unwilling to prevent; 3) involved force that was both proportionate and in accordance with international law; and 4) was exercised by a group of states rather than an individual state. The proposal was attacked on so many fronts that it was quickly withdrawn.

United Nations Secretary General Kofi Annan found himself in a difficult position. His initial reaction to the Kosovo War was to say: 'Emerging slowly, but I believe surely, is an international norm against the violent repression of minorities that will and must take precedence over concerns of State sovereignty.' Later in 1999, however, Annan acknowledged that this norm had not yet achieved legal status and, moreover, that its development could have undesirable consequences for the international order. Annan said: 'What is clear is that enforcement action without Security Council authorization threatens the very core of the international security system founded on the Charter of the UN. Only the Charter provides a universally accepted legal basis for the use of force.' People who, like the Ghanaian-born Secretary General, seek a more peaceful world immediately encounter the dilemma that the constraints imposed by the existing rules on the use of force may – by preventing an unknown number of armed conflicts – already be saving many lives, and that this benefit could be compromised by any attempt to create a new right of unilateral humanitarian action.

To address this dilemma, Canada established an independent body – the International Commission on Intervention and State Sovereignty – and charged it with finding 'some new common ground'. The commissioners, who included former Australian Foreign Minister Gareth Evans, former Philippine President Fidel Ramos, former US Senator Lee Hamilton and the Canadian author Michael Ignatieff, would seem to have disagreed on some of the issues. The resulting report, entitled 'The Responsibility to Protect', contains some passages that favour a right of unilateral humanitarian intervention:

> Based on our reading of state practice, Security Council precedent, established norms, emerging guiding principles, and evolving customary international law, the Commission believes that the Charter's strong bias against military intervention is not to be regarded as absolute when decisive action is required on human protection grounds.

But in their chapter on 'The Question of Authority', the commissioners come to a final conclusion that cuts against this analysis and is distinctly unhelpful to proponents of unilateral humanitarian intervention:

> As a matter of political reality, it would be impossible to find consensus... around any set of proposals for military intervention which acknowledged the validity of any intervention not authorized by the Security Council or General Assembly.

Consensus – or at least very widespread agreement – is a necessary condition for the making or changing of international rules on the use of military force.

Three years later, the commissioners' conclusion was confirmed by another leading group of experts, the UN Secretary

General's High Level Panel on Threats, Challenges and Change. Although the High Level Panel endorsed the concept of the responsibility to protect, it also made clear that, when it comes to the use of military force, the responsibility to protect may only be exercised by the UN Security Council. The Panel proceeded to propose its own series of guidelines, or 'criteria of legitimacy', concerning when force should be used: seriousness of intent, proper purpose, last resort, proportional means and balance of consequences. But the promotion of these criteria was in no way intended to limit the discretionary power of the Council – and only the Council – to deploy force for humanitarian ends.

Although the report of Canada's International Commission was the result of a painful compromise between moral aspiration and political reality, many proponents of unilateral humanitarian intervention – including Lloyd Axworthy, the foreign minister who provided the impetus for the formation of the group – rely upon it readily. Axworthy, in his book *Navigating a New World: Canada's Global Future*, describes the 'gist of the report' as follows:

> [S]overeignty is not a prerogative but a responsibility. It is a way of coming both at the tyrants who hide behind the walls of sovereignty and at those states that can't or won't protect their citizens, without usurping the right of those states that exercise their sovereign duty to care for their people.

Axworthy and most other proponents of the 'responsibility to protect' are motivated by a desire to prevent human suffering. However, by arguing for a new and largely self-judging exception to the UN Charter's prohibition on the use of force, they play into the hands of those who would seek exemption for less benevolent ends.

British Prime Minister Tony Blair has provided the most worrying example of the potential for politically motivated abuse of a right to unilateral humanitarian intervention. In a speech in his Sedgefield constituency in March 2004, he explained how:

[B]efore September 11th, I was already reaching for a different philosophy in international relations from a traditional one that has held sway since the treaty of Westphalia in 1648; namely that a country's internal affairs are for it and you don't interfere unless it threatens you, or breaches a treaty, or triggers an obligation of alliance.

This passage would likely be endorsed by Axworthy and other well-intentioned proponents of the responsibility to protect – were its application left abstract. But Blair proceeded to apply the concept retroactively to Iraq, stating specifically and emphatically: '[W]e surely have a responsibility to act when a nation's people are subjected to a regime such as Saddam's.'

Suddenly, a highly contentious war – justified ostensibly on the basis of a series of UN Security Council resolutions – was being rationalized, one year after the fact, with a doctrine that had already been widely rejected by most of the world's governments. Blair's invocation of a responsibility to protect undoubtedly related back to the all-too-apparent absence of weapons of mass destruction in Iraq, but it was also forward-looking. For Blair – who in his Sedgefield speech claimed almost in passing that existing international law allows for unilateral humanitarian intervention in situations of genocide, mass expulsion and systematic rape – also indicated explicitly a desire to change international law to extend the responsibility to protect to a broader range of circumstances, including tyranny and famine.

The problem with such an objective, of course, is that the many countries that currently oppose a limited right of unilateral humanitarian intervention will oppose, even more strongly, any claim that seeks to go further. Blair, in a truly audacious move, responded to this challenge by seeking to substitute the traditional requirement of state consent in international law-making with the concept of community: 'The essence of a community is common rights and responsibilities. We have obligations in relation to each other. . . . And we do not accept in a community that others have a right to oppress and brutalize their people.' As morally appealing as this approach may be, Blair seemed unable to grasp what it means to live under the rule of law, particularly when the community subject to that law – the international community, in this case – has already established clear and firm rules. In Sedgefield, he went on to say, with no apparent sense of irony:

> I understand the worry the international community has over Iraq. It worries that the US and its allies will, by sheer force of their military might, do whatever they want, unilaterally and without recourse to any rule-based code or doctrine. But our worry is that if the UN – because of a political disagreement in its Councils – is paralysed, then a threat we believe is real will go unchallenged.

This is a vision of power without accountability, exercised by supposedly benevolent leaders with the best interests of their subjects in mind. At the same time, it is reminiscent of a much earlier natural law approach to international law – one that did not require broad-based consent and was instead imposed by the so-called 'civilized'. The prime minister, by reaching for the concept of community, was in fact relying on the international law of the crusaders and conquistadors – which, in essence, was no law at all. Were Blair truly concerned about the plight of the world's oppressed, he would have done better to focus on the other, non-military aspects of the responsibility to protect.

Like the British prime minister, most proponents of the responsibility to protect focus on the concept's potential implications for military intervention. But despite its title, the 'Report of the International Commission on Intervention and State Sovereignty' makes clear that military intervention will only ever be appropriate in 'extreme cases' and that the responsibility to protect encompasses a far broader range of options and obligations. Notable among these is a 'responsibility to prevent' by addressing the 'root causes' of internal conflicts and other threats to civilian populations caused by humans. As the report explains:

> This Commission strongly believes that the responsibility to protect implies an accompanying responsibility to prevent. And we think that it is more than high time for the international community to be doing more to close the gap between rhetorical support for prevention and tangible commitment. The need to do much better on prevention, and to exhaust prevention options before rushing to embrace intervention, were constantly recurring themes in our worldwide consultations, and ones which we wholeheartedly endorse.

The report identifies numerous dimensions to the prevention of root causes. These include support for democratic institutions, press freedom and the rule of law, provision of development assistance and improved terms of trade, and the promotion of arms control, disarmament and nuclear non-proliferation regimes. The overwhelming focus of the responsibility to protect is thus the prevention of conflict through a range of non-military measures that would entail significantly larger transfers of wealth, expertise and opportunity from developed to developing countries. The responsibility to protect entails taking Third World development seriously. From this perspective, any perceived need to engage in humanitarian intervention will usually result from a failure to live up to the responsibility to protect on the part of those who wish to intervene.

It is a reflection of the lack of commitment to this original, broader conception of the responsibility to protect that in April 2004, ten years after the 1994 Rwanda genocide, UN Secretary General Kofi Annan felt it necessary to release a five-point plan for the prevention of similar atrocities in future. The plan emphasizes the main point of the 2001 Report of the International Commission on Intervention and State Sovereignty: that the key to preventing armed conflict and mass atrocities lies in addressing root causes. The Secretary General also recommended that more be done to protect civilians during armed conflict, support the International Criminal Court, and ensure 'early and clear warning' of potential genocides. In July 2004, Annan appointed Argentine law professor Juan Méndez as his Special Adviser on the Prevention of Genocide, assigning him the task of reporting to the Security Council and the General Assembly on unfolding or potential genocides. Finally, as the International Commission on Intervention and State Sovereignty had done, Annan specified that force should only be used as a last resort, and that the instrument for humanitarian intervention must remain the Security Council. He stressed: 'Anyone who embarks on genocide commits a crime against humanity. Humanity must respond by taking action in its own defence. Humanity's instrument for that purpose must be the United Nations, and specifically the Security Council.' This latter point was further reinforced in December 2004, in the Report of the Secretary General's High Level Panel on Threats, Challenges and Change.

In a world where the use of force remains governed by the UN Charter and most countries still believe that the Security Council is functioning appropriately, conflict prevention is the only area where the responsibility to protect could add something new and useful. If developed countries were to redirect just a portion of their current military budgets to foreign aid and development, it should be possible to prevent most armed conflicts and humanitarian crises. In 2003, the United States spent $417 billion on its military, the United Kingdom $37 billion, and the fifteen leading spenders a staggering $723 billion combined. In comparison, the total amount spent on foreign aid by *all* of the world's countries during the same period came to $60 billion, with much of that aid being linked to the purchase of goods and services from donor states, or involving the suspension or cancellation of longstanding foreign debts.

Preventive action taken early will almost always be less expensive than military action taken later. As the International

Commission on Intervention and State Sovereignty explained with regard to the intervention that prompted its own creation and thus the development of the concept of responsibility to protect: 'In Kosovo, almost any kind of preventive activity... would have had to be cheaper than the $46 billion the international community is estimated to have committed at the time of writing in fighting the war and following up with peacekeeping and reconstruction.' The Commission's report was written during the summer and autumn of 2001. Today, the UN Interim Administration Mission in Kosovo retains full authority over the territory with the support of 18,000 NATO-backed peacekeepers and at a massive, ongoing cost to developed states. Worse yet, additional costs are borne indirectly by distressed populations in other needy countries and territories, which, as a result of the redirection of peacekeeping, aid and development budgets to Kosovo, have for five years been deprived essential support. The subsequent interventions in Afghanistan and Iraq have only exacerbated the problem of a seemingly limited pool of money being siphoned from one crisis to another in response to the shifting attentions of Western governments and media. Proponents of the responsibility to protect who focus on military intervention are participating in a terrible charade.

Part Four

International Law during Armed Conflict

Protection of Civilians

More than 300 Iraqi civilians died on 13 February 1991 when two US F-117 stealth bombers targeted the Al'Amiriya bunker in Baghdad. Photographs of the charred and twisted bodies of women and children shocked a world which, thanks to General Norman Schwarzkopf and CNN, had seen little of the horrors of the Gulf War. Pentagon officials, who claimed to have intelligence indicating the bunker was a command and control centre, denied knowledge of the civilian presence. Had they known, the attack would probably have been a war crime.

International humanitarian law – the *jus in bello* – governs *how* wars may be fought. It is distinct from the law governing *when* wars may be fought: the *jus ad bellum* of the UN Charter and self-defence, as discussed in Chapters 1 to 9. Also known as the 'laws of war' or the 'law of armed conflict', international humanitarian law seeks to limit the human suffering that is the inevitable consequence of war. As a body of law, it traces its origins to 1859, when the Swiss businessman Henri Dunant witnessed the aftermath of the Franco-Austrian Battle of Solferino – in which 40,000 men died, many as the result of untreated wounds – and initiated a movement that became the International Committee of the Red Cross (ICRC).

Today, the rules of international humanitarian law are found primarily in the four Geneva Conventions of 1949 (and the predecessor Hague Conventions of 1907). The Geneva Conventions are aimed at protecting, respectively: the wounded and sick on land; the wounded, sick and shipwrecked at sea; prisoners of war; and civilians (who are technically referred to as 'non-combatants').

The protections guaranteed under these treaties are replicated and elaborated in two Additional Protocols of 1977, a multitude of more specific treaties and a parallel body of unwritten customary international law.

A key principle of international humanitarian law prohibits the direct targeting of civilians, as Article 51(2) of Additional Protocol I explains:

> The civilian population as such, as well as individual civilians, shall not be the object of attack. Acts or threats of violence the primary purpose of which is to spread terror among the civilian population are prohibited.

In addition to its presence in this widely ratified treaty, the rule against the direct targeting of civilians during armed conflict is generally considered to have achieved the status of customary international law, and therefore binds all countries, including those that have not ratified the relevant conventions, treaties and protocols.

It follows that civilians cannot be collectively punished. The actions of US forces in Fallujah, Iraq, in April 2004, following the killing and mutilation of four US contractors, certainly looked like war crimes from afar. Hundreds of civilians were killed, many of them with apparent indiscrimination, as US marines fought their way into the densely populated city – before retreating out of concern about US public opinion, and popular uprisings around Iraq provoked by Arab news reports of the many innocents killed. Immediately after the US presidential election on 2 November 2004, the marines moved back into Fallujah with a vengeance. Howitzers and 2000-pound bombs, neither of which are particularly precise weapons, were used to soften up the city. Fuel-air explosives were dropped on residential neighbourhoods and virtually every house was struck by US tank, machine-gun or rifle fire.

Even if the assault on Fallujah was not motivated by revenge, it appears to have been an illegally indiscriminate attack – because all reasonable measures were not taken to avoid harming civilians. The 'carpet bombing' of North Vietnam in the early 1970s was a violation of international humanitarian law, as were moves to designate certain villages as 'free-fire zones', as was famously the case at the village of My Lai in 1968 when 300 civilians were massacred by US soldiers. Iraq violated the same rule when it fired eleven Scud missiles at Israel during the 1991 Gulf War. The Scuds, notoriously inaccurate to begin with, were rendered even more inaccurate by modifications that were designed to extend their range. They were aimed at the general vicinity of Tel Aviv, rather than at specific military targets, and their use justifiably provoked outrage. The use of B-52 bombers to lay down swathes of destruction in the Basra area of Iraq in 1991 was probably not a war crime because the bombing was directed solely against the Iraqi Republican Guard, though the International Committee of the Red Cross and Human Rights Watch have concluded otherwise.

Given the indiscriminate character of the assault on Fallujah, the duty to protect civilians was probably also violated when US forces refused to allow men between the ages of fifteen and forty-five to leave the city before the attack. Hundreds if not thousands of innocents may have perished as a result, not just of the attacks, but of the discrimination on the basis of sex and age that put them in harm's way. The United States continued to violate international humanitarian law, as it and its allies have done throughout the Iraq War and occupation, by refusing to count and document the Iraqi dead. According to the *New York Times*, the first goal of the November 2004 assault on Fallujah was to capture the city's general hospital because 'the American military believed that it was the source of rumours about heavy casualties' and 'this time around, the American military intends to fight its own information war, countering or squelching what has become one of the insurgents' most potent weapons'. Article 16 of the First Geneva Convention of 1949 is categorical with regard to the relevant obligation: 'Parties to the conflict shall record as soon as possible, in respect of each wounded, sick or dead person of the adverse Party falling into their hands, any particulars which may assist in his identification...[and] shall prepare...certificates of death or duly authenticated lists of the dead.' The same rule exists as part of customary international law. Here, and in too many other circumstances, the United States, Britain and Australia are committing war crimes that they could easily avoid.

Civilians are neither members of the armed forces of a 'belligerent' (that is to say, a party to the conflict), nor do they play a direct or active part in the hostilities. A contractor who delivers ammunition to combatants is actively taking part in hostilities, but what about one who is merely delivering food, water or sanitary supplies? If the same contractor is alternating between delivering ammunition and delivering food, he or she is not a civilian, just like the person who fights by night and pretends to be a non-combatant by day.

International humanitarian law seeks to draw the clearest possible distinction between combatants and civilians. In order to be considered soldiers, individuals should be in a chain of command, wear identifiable insignia, carry their weapons openly, and act in accordance with the laws of war. The sanction for non-compliance with these requirements is the loss, if captured, of 'prisoner of war' status and the standards of treatment it requires. The rationale is that individuals who do not fight fairly – wearing uniforms, carrying their weapons openly, etc. – do not deserve the protection of the rules. The distinction simultaneously rewards soldiers for being readily identifiable and deters civilians from entering the fray, thereby keeping the line between combatants and civilians as discernible as possible and maximizing civilian safety.

Mercenaries – persons who fight solely for financial gain – are not entitled to be treated as prisoners of war. The increasing use of private contractors by the US military, in some cases very near or even in combat zones, raises questions as to what, if any, rights – beyond international human rights – these individuals have if captured by opposing armies. At the same time, the extended involvement of these contractors in activities traditionally reserved to military personnel is obfuscating the all-important distinction between combatants and civilians, with potentially serious consequences. Journalists, for instance, are considered civilians even when 'embedded' within armed units, provided they do not themselves take up arms. Journalists may not be targeted by military forces, though they put themselves at risk of being accidentally or incidentally harmed whenever they approach or enter a combat zone. The risk to journalists has increased in proportion to the growth in numbers of militarily active contractors wearing civilian clothes, since enemy forces cannot readily distinguish one group from the other.

Balancing 'military necessity' against the protection of civilians is seldom easy, either for targeting or choosing weapons. However, some general constraints remain: attacks must be deliberate and tend towards the military defeat of the enemy; they must not cause harm to civilians or civilian objects that is excessive in relation to the direct military advantage anticipated; and military necessity does not justify violating other rules of international humanitarian law. Usually, the boundary between acceptable and unacceptable targets will depend on the facts of the specific situation. For example, the tower of a mosque is normally inviolable, since places of worship and cultural property enjoy special protection, but may become a legitimate target if used by a sniper. Although balancing military necessity against risks to civilians is always required, international humanitarian law accepts that wars are fought to be won, while containing belligerents within a sphere of (relatively) civilized behaviour.

During the 1991 Gulf War, these obligations were taken seriously. Desert Storm was the first major combat operation undertaken by the United States after the Vietnam War. Fearful of another domestic backlash if things went wrong, the politicians left the conduct of hostilities to professional soldiers – who are trained to fight by the book. Adherence to the rule of law was further aided by the fact that the United States was part of a substantial coalition. Some allies of the United States accord considerable importance to the requirements of international humanitarian law, and so, in order to maintain the coalition, the United States had to fight according to the rules.

Some 200 US military lawyers were dispatched to the Gulf. Legal experts vetted every targeting decision. A strike on a statue of Saddam Hussein in Baghdad was ruled out on the basis that only targets that contribute to the war effort are permissible under international humanitarian law. Those legal controversies that arose stemmed from differing interpretations of the law, rather than any desire to ignore legal constraints. At least five British officers resigned their commissions after the United States used cluster bombs and fuel-air explosives to attack Iraqi weaponry, with devastating effects on enemy soldiers. A similar divergence of views arose over the use of earthmovers and tank-mounted ploughs to bury Iraqi soldiers alive in their trenches, thus avoiding the dangers of hand-to-hand combat. International humanitarian law forbids methods of warfare that cause 'unnecessary suffering or superfluous injury', but where one sets the balance between military necessity and humanitarian concerns also depends, perhaps inevitably, on where one is coming from – during the 1990s, the US government was particularly concerned to avoid American casualties.

After decades of massive defence spending, the United States is today assured of victory in any war it chooses to fight. High-tech weaponry has reduced the dangers to US personnel, making it easier to sell war to domestic constituencies. As a result, some US politicians had begun – at least until the quagmire in Iraq – to view armed conflict as an attractive foreign policy option in times of domestic scandal or economic decline, rather than the high-risk recourse of last resort. This change in thinking has led to a more cavalier approach to the *jus ad bellum*, as exemplified by the Bush Doctrine of pre-emptive self-defence, and is beginning to have a similar effect on the *jus in bello*. When war is seen as a tool of foreign policy – Clausewitz's 'politics by other means' – political and financial considerations may distort the balance between military necessity and humanitarian concerns.

In Washington, it has become accepted wisdom that future opponents are unlikely to abide by international humanitarian law. This assumption has been fuelled by events. During the 1991 Gulf War, captured American pilots were brutalized in several ways, some having been raped. The September 2001 attacks on the Twin Towers breached international humanitarian law as 'crimes against humanity', a category of international criminal law that concerns violent acts committed as part of systematic attacks on civilian populations. And during the 2003 war, Iraqi soldiers committed the war crime of 'perfidy' by using civilian clothes and white flags to trick and then kill opposing forces. If your enemy is going to cheat, why bother playing by the rules?

No love has been lost between Defense Secretary Donald Rumsfeld and his military lawyers. In October 2002, CIA operatives used an unmanned Predator reconnaissance aircraft to track the Taliban leader Mullah Omar to a building in a residential area of Kabul. The air strike to kill Omar was called off because a lawyer at US Central Command was concerned about the risk of disproportionate civilian casualties. According to a report in the *New Yorker*, the incident left Rumsfeld 'kicking a lot of glass and breaking doors'. The Secretary sought – unsuccessfully – to reduce the number of lawyers in uniform.

Rumsfeld also encouraged a re-evaluation of the prohibition on targeting civilians, particularly with regard to actions directed at shattering support for opponent regimes. This kind of thinking was popular during the Second World War – as evidenced by the firebombing of Dresden, Hamburg and several cities in Japan – but was subsequently rejected during the negotiation of the 1949 Geneva Conventions. In the last several years, a theory claiming that every regime has 'five strategic rings' has attracted adherents in Washington. According to this view, each ring represents a different facet of a society: political leadership, economic system, supporting infrastructure, population and military forces. Air power is supposed to enable the United States to target opponents from the 'inside out', bypassing military forces and attacking the political leadership directly. In this context, the indirect harm caused to civilians – through the destruction of bridges, electrical grids, oil refineries and water-filtration plants – is considered justified because it promotes dissatisfaction within the regime and thus hastens the course of the conflict (while, incidentally, reducing the cost of victory).

During the 1991 Gulf War, the United States targeted the Iraqi national electrical grid, shutting down hospitals as well as water and sewage stations. The health consequences for civilians were severe, but the strikes were legal because Iraqi military communications depended heavily on the grid. In 1999, when Slobodan Milošević's forces proved much more resilient than expected, the United States pushed for the adoption of a looser approach, which led to the use of more questionable military tactics. Electrical grids and water-filtration plants in Serbia were targeted, not to disrupt the actions of the Yugoslav Army in Kosovo but to provoke domestic opposition to Milošević's government in Belgrade.

Equally problematic was the targeting of the State Serbian Television and Radio station in April 1999, as well as the Iraqi State Television station in March 2003. The two stations were legitimate targets if they had been integrated into military communications networks, but not if they were simply being used for propaganda. Again, applying the rules often has as much to do with finer points of fact as it does with those of law.

In 1991, a number of coalition warplanes (especially British Tornados) were lost to Iraqi anti-aircraft fire because they were bombing from low altitudes in order to reduce civilian casualties. Less accurate high-altitude strikes by B-52s were restricted to targets well clear of civilian areas. Almost all the bombing during the Kosovo War was carried out above the reach of Serbian air defences. As a result of the high altitudes, NATO pilots were sometimes unable to distinguish between military and civilian targets, with disastrous results for several refugee convoys. Again, as a result of the United States taking a somewhat different approach to these issues, there is now a different reckoning of the balance between military necessity and humanitarian concerns.

The Kosovo War was complicated by the fact that Yugoslavia had ratified Additional Protocol I, which imposes stricter protections for civilians than the Geneva Conventions. Since the United States was the only member of NATO not to have ratified the Protocol, and therefore not bound to uphold its standards reciprocally vis-à-vis Yugoslavia, certain types of missions were allocated only to US pilots. Canadian pilots, who train with their American counterparts, were not assigned as wingmen to US pilots in missions over the former Yugoslavia: the Canadian pilots could not be relied upon to respond to some threats, such as anti-aircraft fire coming from a school or hospital, in the same way that US pilots would. Whether countries such as Canada and Britain are collectively liable under Protocol I for the actions of US pilots operating under NATO targeting procedures remains an open question. Carla Del Ponte, the prosecutor for the International Criminal Tribunal for the former Yugoslavia, chose not to investigate any of NATO's alleged war crimes. The issue did not arise in Iraq in 2003, since Saddam never ratified Protocol I.

Precision-guided missiles give rise to a further complication. When civilians are present, international humanitarian law requires belligerents to use weapons that can distinguish between civilians and combatants; it follows that they should usually use the most accurate weapons available to them. In another instance of political and financial cost-benefit analysis intruding into international humanitarian law, the United States argues that this requirement imposes an unfair burden on it, given the substantial production costs of smart bombs. Extending the same logic, it could be argued that, because precision-guided weapons reduce the number of civilian casualties across a campaign, attacking forces using them may exercise less concern for the protection of civilians when making individual targeting decisions, since the overall collateral damage will still be less than in a low-tech war.

Applying such calculations to rules designed to protect human beings is not only inappropriate, but also immoral.

The use of weapons that cause superfluous injury or unnecessary suffering is also prohibited under international humanitarian law. Explosive or expanding ('dum-dum') bullets, booby-traps and blinding laser weapons are banned outright on the basis that the military benefits of their use can never be proportionate to the suffering they cause. A special treaty – the 1925 Geneva Protocol – unequivocally prohibits the use of poisonous gas and biological weapons. These prohibitions have achieved the status of customary international law, as was confirmed by the harshly negative reaction of other countries to the use of nerve and mustard gas during the Iran–Iraq War of the 1980s. Other weapons have been banned by most but not all countries. The United States' refusal to ratify the 1997 Ottawa Landmines Convention can create awkward situations for its allies. In 2001, Canadian soldiers operating in Afghanistan were ordered by their US commander to lay mines around their camp. When the Canadians refused to do so, US soldiers, who were not subject to the same restrictions, laid the mines. Depleted uranium, cluster bombs and fuel-air explosives are among the weapons whose use remains legally uncertain. Favoured for their armour-piercing abilities, depleted uranium shells leave radioactive residues that can pose health problems for civilians and combatants alike. Given the scientific uncertainty as to the extent of the risk, humanitarian concerns should prevail – though depleted uranium was used extensively in Iraq in 2003 (as, indeed, were cluster bombs). Again, political and financial expediency have seemingly influenced the balance between humanitarianism and military necessity, at least for the United States.

Nuclear weapons are not banned but their use is subject to the constraints of international humanitarian law. Although it is difficult to envision how the use of nuclear weapons could not cause suffering disproportionate to military gain, the Pentagon in March 2002 issued a *Nuclear Posture Review* that cited the need for new nuclear weapons specifically designed to destroy deeply buried command centres and biological weapon facilities. In February 2003, the British Defence Secretary Geoff Hoon stated that Britain reserved the right to use nuclear weapons against Iraq in 'extreme self-defence'. Hoon sought to justify his assertion on the basis of a 1996 advisory opinion of the International Court of Justice in which the Court could not 'conclude definitively whether the threat or use of nuclear weapons would be lawful or unlawful in an extreme circumstance of self-defence, in which the very survival of a state would be at stake'. But Hoon omitted to mention the latter part of this passage, which (as quoted here) clearly shows that his reliance on the opinion was misplaced. The only state whose survival was at stake in February 2003 was Iraq.

Hoon's advisers would have done better to direct him to the rules concerning belligerent reprisals. Actions that violate international humanitarian law (though not acts that violate the *jus ad bellum*) can become legally justifiable when taken in response to violations of the law by the other side. The purpose of belligerent reprisals is to deter further violations, and the possibility of reprisal is often cited as the reason countries comply with international humanitarian law. But belligerent reprisals must be proportionate to the original violation and cannot be directed towards civilians or objects indispensable to the survival of civilians. The apparently indiscriminate targeting of civilians in Fallujah, Iraq, in April 2004 – after the killing and mutilation of four US contractors – could not be legally justified, even as a belligerent reprisal.

No treaty specifically prohibits belligerent reprisals carried out with otherwise prohibited weapons. This raises the possibility that it might be legal to use nuclear weapons in response to the use of chemical or biological weapons. In 1991, then US Secretary of State James Baker privately warned Saddam Hussein that any recourse to chemical or biological weapons would result in a tactical nuclear response by the United States. More recently, the Bush Administration has shown no compunction about making the threat publicly. *The National Strategy to Combat Weapons of*

Mass Destruction, released in December 2002, 'reserves the right to respond with overwhelming force – including through resort to all of our options – to the use of WMD against the United States, our forces abroad, and friends and allies'. But the use of any nuclear weapon, even as a belligerent reprisal, would almost certainly cause disproportionate civilian suffering and thus violate international humanitarian law.

The military power of the United States prevailed in the Iraq War. A number of reluctant allies were pressured into providing practical and political support. Many critics of the invasion – and of the United States' conduct during it – were initially silenced, not just by the victory but because only a few thousand civilians had been killed. But balancing military necessity and humanitarian concerns was never the exclusive province of Donald Rumsfeld and like-minded advisers such as Paul Wolfowitz. Most international humanitarian law treaties contain something called the Martens Clause, which in its original form was drafted by the Russian delegate to the conferences that produced the Hague Conventions of 1907:

Until a more complete code of the laws of war is issued, the high contracting Parties think it right to declare that in cases not included in the Regulations adopted by them, populations and belligerents remain under the protection and empire of the principles of international law, as they result from the usages established between civilized nations, from the laws of humanity, and the requirements of the public conscience.

International humanitarian law is, in part, what you and I and the rest of the people on this planet determine it to be. In the lead-up to future wars – and throughout the ongoing occupation of Iraq – we should insist that all countries uphold the strict standards of international humanitarian law, not because it is expedient but because it is right.

Protection of Combatants and Prisoners of War

Soldiers are legitimate targets during armed conflict. Killing members of the enemy's armed forces is one of the goals of military action. Still, soldiers – referred to under international humanitarian law as 'combatants' – benefit from some protections, including the prohibition on the use of certain types of weapons discussed in the previous chapter. The proscription of chemical and biological weapons benefits combatants as well as civilians, as does the ban on booby-traps, the developing ban on anti-personnel landmines set out in the 1997 Ottawa Landmines Convention, and the limitations on the use of nuclear weapons. The prohibitions on explosive or expanding bullets and blinding laser weapons are directed more specifically at protecting soldiers, as is the requirement that soldiers who have been wounded or wish to surrender must be captured rather than killed.

Soldiers who have been wounded are deemed *hors de combat* (out of combat) and accorded protections similar to those that apply to civilians. Soldiers who lay down their arms or otherwise clearly express 'an intention to surrender' become prisoners of war. Wounded soldiers and prisoners of war cannot be killed, used as human shields, held hostage, or used to clear landmines. The execution-style shooting of a wounded and unarmed Iraqi in Fallujah in November 2004, as captured on tape by an embedded television cameraman, was almost certainly a war crime.

Medical personnel benefit from similarly strict protections, while medical facilities, ambulances and hospital ships are off-limits as targets unless used as locations from which to launch attacks. As with many rules of international humanitarian law, this rule is sometimes honoured in the breach. In 1992 and early 1993, the main hospital in Sarajevo, Bosnia-Herzegovina, was hit by no less than 172 mortar shells while full of patients.

Civilians can be protected in time of armed conflict only if a distinction is maintained between combatants and non-combatants. This differentiation is achieved by offering combatants the protection of prisoner of war status if captured, as long as they are in a chain of command, wearing a fixed distinctive emblem (usually a shoulder patch), carrying their arms openly and acting in accordance with international humanitarian law. These incentives are not always effective, especially in conflicts involving irregular forces in poorer countries, and some experts argue that the distinctive emblem requirement is inconsistent with modern forms of war. Apart from their turbans, the armed forces of the Taliban government did not wear anything approaching uniforms during the 2001 Afghanistan War, though they were in a chain of command, carried their arms openly and, for the most part, abided by international humanitarian law.

The distinction between combatants and non-combatants is most severely threatened by the practice of US special forces, who constitute an increasingly important part of the US military yet have – with the apparent support of Secretary of Defense Donald Rumsfeld – taken to wearing civilian clothing. The practice has been challenged. When the New Zealand government sent a contingent of commandos to fight in Afghanistan, it refused to allow the soldiers to wear civilian clothes, a decision that created some friction with the United States. The decision was correct: if special forces – indeed, any soldiers – are captured operating out of uniform, they are not entitled to the protections owed to prisoners of war regardless of the country for which they fight. Although this consequence may seem unduly harsh, it is based on the rationale that soldiers who do not wear their uniforms are not fighting fairly, and are needlessly endangering civilians, and consequently do not deserve the full protections of international humanitarian law. The policy of allowing US special forces to wear civilian clothes entails unnecessary risks for individual soldiers and civilians; perhaps in recognition of this, the practice – at least in Afghanistan – has since been reversed.

Rumsfeld's disdain for international humanitarian law became blatantly apparent in January 2002 when suspected Taliban and al-Qaeda members were transported to the US naval base in Guantánamo Bay, Cuba. Ignoring public criticism from a number of European leaders, the UN High Commissioner for Human Rights and even the normally neutral and extraordinarily discrete International Committee of the Red Cross, the Secretary of Defense insisted the detainees were not prisoners of war and refused to convene the tribunals required under Article 5 of the Third Geneva Convention relative to the Treatment of Prisoners of War to determine their status. Rumsfeld also ignored advice from the Pentagon's own lawyers, the 'judge advocates', and based his decision on an analysis of international humanitarian law by then White House Counsel (now Attorney General) Alberto Gonzales, a former corporate lawyer from Texas. Three years after the war in Afghanistan, nearly 600 suspects remain at Guantánamo Bay despite having never been charged or granted access to counsel. Only forty-two detainees have been released, including five Saudis who were traded for six Britons (and one Belgian) who had been arrested and tortured in Riyadh. More than thirty detainees have attempted suicide.

In November 2002, the English Court of Appeal correctly described the position of the Guantánamo Bay detainees as 'legally objectionable'; it was as if they were in a 'legal black hole'. The situation has improved marginally since then. On 29 June 2004, the US Supreme Court finally addressed the matter. On behalf of a 6–3 majority of judges, Justice John Paul Stevens wrote:

> Executive imprisonment has been considered oppressive and lawless since John, at Runnymede, pledged that no free man should be imprisoned, dispossessed, outlawed, or exiled save by

the judgment of his peers or by the law of the land. The judges of England developed the writ of habeas corpus largely to preserve these immunities from executive restraint.

Stevens went on to hold that anyone detained by the US government outside the United States has the right to have the legal basis for his detention reviewed by a US federal court. Just one week later, the Pentagon announced that it would in fact convene the status determination tribunals required by Article 5 of the Third Geneva Convention.

These Article 5 tribunals are not courts, but rather panels of three US military officers who review the facts pertaining to each detainee and determine whether he or she is a prisoner of war. The detainees are not provided access to lawyers. Instead, military officers are assigned as their 'personal representatives'. The absence of legal counsel and the non-judicial nature of the process probably fail to meet the standards of due process envisaged by the Supreme Court in its June 2004 decision. The matter is now the subject of a new round of litigation and the Supreme Court may eventually rule further. The Bush Administration's belated move to respect the Third Geneva Convention is nothing more than an attempt to buy more time to interrogate the Guantánamo Bay detainees outside the constraints of domestic and international law.

The Article 5 status determination tribunals are different from the military commission concurrently established to criminally prosecute three of the detainees at Guantánamo Bay. This military commission, and other commissions to come, are the result of a November 2001 presidential order. The order permits the US military to create the commissions to try detainees and authorizes the imposition of the death penalty when all three of the military officers who serve like judges agree. The commissions apply procedures similar to regular military courts, albeit with tighter controls on the release of evidence to defence counsel and journalists. The accused is provided with lawyers, or may engage his own. The presumption of innocence applies, as does the usual burden of proof, namely 'guilty beyond a reasonable doubt'. However, the Third Geneva Convention stipulates that POWs must, if charged with crimes, be tried in the regular military courts of the detaining country. The operation of the status determination tribunals could thus, by determining that individual detainees are POWs, remove them from the purview – and relative secrecy – of the military commissions. This possible consequence helps explain Rumsfeld's refusal to create such tribunals in January 2002. How one views the situation will depend on whether one trusts the US government to play it straight with intelligence, and treat detainees fairly, even behind closed doors.

Widespread violations of international humanitarian law have been committed against detainees in Afghanistan and Iraq. In November 2001, a prisoner revolt at Mazar-i-Sharif was put down with air-to-surface missiles and B-52 launched bombs. More than 175 detainees were killed; fifty died with their hands tied behind their backs. In December 2002, the *Washington Post* reported on the use of 'stress and duress' techniques during interrogations at Bagram air base in Afghanistan. In March 2003, the *New York Times* reported that, while in custody over a three-month period, a suspected member of al-Qaeda was 'fed very little, while being subjected to sleep and light deprivation, prolonged isolation and room temperatures that varied from 100 degrees to 10 degrees'. Ten degrees Fahrenheit is easily cold enough to kill. Also in March 2003, the *New York Times* reported that a death certificate, signed by a US military pathologist, stated the cause of death of a twenty-two-year-old Afghan detainee at Bagram air base in December 2002 as 'blunt force injuries to lower extremities complicating coronary artery disease'. The form gave the pathologist four choices for 'mode of death': 'natural, accident, suicide, homicide'. She marked the box for homicide. A week earlier, another Afghan detainee – just thirty years old – had reportedly died of a pulmonary embolism.

In July 2003, UN Secretary General Kofi Annan reported to the Security Council that his Special Representative for Iraq, the late Sergio Vieira de Mello, had expressed concern to the United States and Britain about their treatment of thousands of detained Iraqis. One week later, Amnesty International claimed that US forces in Iraq were resorting to 'prolonged sleep deprivation, prolonged restraint in painful positions – sometimes combined with exposure to loud music, prolonged hooding and exposure to bright lights'.

Regrettably, the reports failed to attract widespread media attention until March 2004, when it became known that the *New Yorker* was about to publish photographs of prisoner abuse at Abu Ghraib prison near Baghdad, together with a damning report by investigative journalist Seymour Hersh. At this point, CBS television decided to air photographs it had been suppressing for several weeks, reportedly at the behest of the Bush Administration. The photographs showed detainees stripped naked, ridiculed, piled on top of each other, being raped, forced to masturbate, bitten by dogs, and terrorized with the threat of electrocution. The actions were blatant violations of both international humanitarian law and the detainees' international human rights.

Given the proximity to the 2003 Iraq War, it is likely that some of the detainees at Abu Ghraib were prisoners of war. If so, the captors who abused them violated the Third Geneva Convention, Article 13 of which provides that POWs 'must at all times be protected, particularly against acts of violence or intimidation and against insults and public curiosity'. To reinforce the point, Article 14 stipulates that prisoners of war 'are entitled in all circumstances to respect for their persons and their honour'.

Any of the captives at Abu Ghraib who were not prisoners of war were probably still protected by Common Article 3 of the Geneva Conventions. This provision requires that, even in armed conflicts not of an international character (as, arguably, the situation in Iraq had become), persons taking no part in the hostilities are protected absolutely from 'violence to life and person, in particular murder of all kinds, mutilation, cruel treatment and torture' as well as 'outrages upon personal dignity, in particular, humiliating and degrading treatment'. (The first part of Common Article 3 is reproduced in Chapter 5.)

Regardless of the status of the detainees, some of the outrages committed against them were violations of the 1984 Convention against Torture and Other Cruel, Inhuman or Degrading Treatment or Punishment, a treaty ratified by the United States and universally regarded as codifying customary international law. Article 1 of the Convention defines torture as:

[A]ny act by which severe pain or suffering, whether physical or mental, is intentionally inflicted on a person for such purposes as obtaining from him or a third person information or a confession, punishing him for an act he or a third person has committed or is suspected of having committed, or intimidating or coercing him or a third person, or for any reason based on discrimination of any kind, when such pain or suffering is inflicted by or at the instigation of or with the consent or acquiescence of a public official or other person acting in an official capacity.

A confidential memorandum, prepared for Secretary of Defense Rumsfeld by a group of Bush Administration lawyers in March 2003 and obtained by the *Washington Post* in June 2004, argued that the President was not bound by the provisions of the Third Geneva Convention or the Convention against Torture, at least insofar as these international rules are implemented in US domestic law. The analysis was based on an earlier Department of Justice memorandum that made a series of dubious assumptions – including that none of the detainees were prisoners of war and that customary international law and US federal law are hermetically sealed from each other – that together transformed legal analysis into an exercise in politically motivated justification. That memorandum was written by John Yoo, a political appointee who has since returned to his regular position as a law professor at the University of California, Berkeley. The *New York Times* reported that the State Department Legal Adviser, William Taft IV, dissented from the group's analysis and its conclusions, 'warning that such a position would weaken the protections of the Geneva Conventions for American troops'.

The abuse of detainees engages the responsibility not only of individual soldiers. Under a principle of international criminal law known as 'command responsibility', individuals higher in the chain of command – including defence secretaries and presidents who serve as commanders-in-chief – may also commit war crimes if they know, or have reason to know, that their subordinates are committing or are about to commit crimes and fail to take all feasible steps to prevent or stop the violations. Article 12 of the Third Geneva Convention provides but one articulation of the principle:

> Prisoners of war are in the hands of the enemy Power, but not of the individuals or military units who have captured them. Irrespective of the individual responsibilities that may exist, the Detaining Power is responsible for the treatment given them.

Additional violations of international humanitarian law were committed when the International Committee of the Red Cross was denied access to some parts of Abu Ghraib prison, and to some detainees, as reportedly occurred early in 2004. Under the 1949 Geneva Conventions and the 1977 Additional Protocols, the ICRC is mandated to visit and register prisoners of war. This right of access is essential because it promotes the good treatment of prisoners of war and ensures they do not disappear. Although the ICRC traditionally does not publicly denounce governments that fail to uphold international humanitarian law – in order to preserve its neutrality, thereby ensuring future access to prisoners and civilians in need – it has, on several occasions since 2001, openly expressed concern about the actions of the United States.

Many of the ICRC's concerns persist today with regard to persons detained by the United States or its allies in a variety of known and unknown locations, including in Afghanistan and at a US airbase on the British-owned Indian Ocean island of Diego Garcia. The ICRC has not been provided access to these individuals – itself a violation – and there is no way of knowing whether they are being tortured, otherwise mistreated, or killed.

In the same context, a second confidential memorandum obtained by the *Washington Post* in October 2004 was reportedly used to justify a related war crime: the transfer of detainees out of occupied Iraq for interrogation elsewhere. Article 49 of the Fourth Geneva Convention protects civilians during an occupation by unambiguously prohibiting 'individual or mass forcible transfers, as well as deportation of protected persons from occupied territory ... regardless of their motive'. Indeed, one of the principal purposes of the Fourth Geneva Convention is to prevent persons from being moved out of an occupied territory and thus out of the oversight of the International Committee of the Red Cross. The memorandum, which strains legal credulity, was written by Jack Goldsmith, who served as a political appointee at the Pentagon and Department of Justice, and is now a professor of law at Harvard University.

Even alleged terrorists are protected by the ban on extra-judicial killing found in numerous human rights treaties and customary international law. When it comes to extra-judicial killings, George W. Bush's State of the Union address in January 2003 included a damning admission: 'All told, more than 3,000 suspected terrorists have been arrested in many countries. Many others have met a different fate. Let's put it this way – they are no longer a problem to the United States and our friends and allies.' Previous administrations at least paid lip service to the existence of normative constraints by concealing and denying their covert operations. The Bush Administration, during its more arrogant moments, lets the mask slip – to the discredit of the nation and, by undermining the already fragile edifice of international humanitarian law, at the peril of the individual soldiers whom so many of the rules are designed to protect.

War Crimes Courts and Tribunals

'This is theatre. Bush is the real criminal.'

With a smile, Saddam Hussein, looking fit and well groomed despite nearly seven months of interrogations and solitary confinement, condemned the Iraqi Special Tribunal established to try him and senior members of his regime for alleged atrocities. Saddam's allegations of political bias resonate deeply. During a television interview shortly after his capture, President George W. Bush stated: 'He is a torturer, a murderer, and they had rape rooms, and this is a disgusting tyrant who deserves justice, the ultimate justice.'

Dishevelled, confused and compliant when captured in December 2003, Saddam must have seemed the perfect puppet for an election-year show trial. Salem Chalabi, the nephew of the once omnipresent and now discredited Iraqi opposition leader Ahmad Chalabi, was handpicked by US envoy L. Paul Bremer to direct the production. A statute for the tribunal was quickly drafted, drawing heavily on the Rome Statute of the International Criminal Court; a slate of safely anti-Saddam judges was rubber-stamped by Bremer's Iraqi Governing Council. The FBI was assigned to gather evidence; twenty US lawyers were dispatched to support the prosecution. After the Governing Council had been hastily transformed into a supposedly sovereign interim government in June 2004, one of its first acts was to reintroduce the death penalty. Only the resurgent and all-too-predictable resilience of Saddam, the hardened dictator, frustrated the careful preparations.

Saddam's transfer to Iraqi authorities and his first court appearance on 1 July 2004 were small concessions to international law: the Third Geneva Convention requires that prisoners of war be either charged or released at the end of hostilities. Bush, citing security concerns, initially resisted transferring custody over Saddam to the Iraqi interim government, but was soon reminded that unnecessary violations of the Geneva Conventions can lead to diplomatic trouble – not to mention judicial review by the newly vigilant US Supreme Court. And so Saddam and eleven other senior Iraqi officials were handed over, though, as with the transfer of sovereignty, the transfer was formal rather than practical. Saddam and his henchmen remain under US lock and key. The only print journalists allowed to attend the hearing were American. Al-Jazeera and CNN were permitted to film the event – carefully timed to coincide with prime-time breakfast television stateside – but had to block out the sound of Saddam's voice.

At first it seemed that Saddam might be denied the right to choose his own lawyers, especially after his senior wife, Sajidah, assembled a multinational legal defence team, some of whom wanted to put the United States on trial. There were no defence lawyers in the courtroom during Saddam's first appearance before the tribunal. The president of the tribunal, Salem Chalabi, even raised the possibility of holding the trial in secret, but this measure would have too clearly exposed the bias of the proceedings. The impropriety of the Iraqi court is not its capacity to determine and apply the law, as international human rights organizations were quick to assert. Not only does the statute of the new tribunal take the bulk of its provisions directly from the governing instrument of the International Criminal Court; international experts could be provided to assist the judges, prosecution and defence. Carefully selected Iraqi jurists could, with time and patience, grasp the intricacies of international criminal law and apply them to complex facts. Rather, the problems with using an Iraqi tribunal to try the former dictator concern inadvertent bias, the likelihood of rushed procedures, and the absence of international legitimacy.

As with most members of the Iraqi Governing Council and interim government, the judges of the tribunal will have suffered as a result of Saddam's actions; few Iraqis escaped the shadow of his rule. The inexorable conflict between judicial functions and personal interests has led most of the world's legal systems to preclude victims acting as judges or jurors. While we grieve with victims and families, we would not wish them to determine guilt.

As for speed, one member of the Iraqi Governing Council indicated initially that Saddam's trial might start within weeks of his capture. At the time, others spoke of a conviction in June 2004. It now seems likely that proceedings will begin in 2005. Iraqis are accustomed to swift justice. During Saddam's rule, trials – if held at all – rarely took more than a day. Yet the evidence against Saddam is voluminous. The final charge sheet could contain tens of thousands of crimes, including murder, torture, mass rape, armed aggression, using chemical weapons, mistreating prisoners of war, and perhaps even genocide. Some 50,000 people died in Saddam's 1988 campaign against the Kurds, during which chemical weapons were used on at least sixty occasions. Rooms full of documents will need to be read and a multitude of victims and witnesses will wish to testify. Mounting a rigorous defence will be an awesomely difficult, time-consuming task. Yet a rigorous defence there must be. By providing due process to those individuals accused of the most heinous crimes, societies demonstrate their adherence to the rule of law and the rightness of the punishments they mete. Establishing Saddam's guilt beyond a reasonable doubt also serves an important policy purpose, in that an undeniably fair trial might help sway people whose sympathy he would otherwise attract. Countless dissatisfied young men and women across the Islamic world will be watching the proceedings closely; if the trial were patently fair, they might be less inclined towards violent acts.

The most significant problem with the Iraqi tribunal is that it lacks the legitimacy of an international court. International criminal law is designed to provide accountability for particularly grave offences – and access to justice for the victims – when national legal systems are unable or unwilling to act. The potential charges against Saddam are proscribed by treaty and custom. They are international crimes in both severity and scope: the victims of his regime include the thousands of people tortured and killed during the Iraqi occupation of Kuwait, and the hundreds of thousands who died or were maimed during Iraq's decade-long war with Iran. These are crimes giving rise to universal jurisdiction in the national courts of other countries, and, on the basis of treaties or resolutions of the UN Security Council, to the jurisdiction of international courts and tribunals.

The higher the office of the alleged offender, and the more serious his crimes, the more appropriate an international judicial forum becomes. The multinational Nuremberg Tribunal was used for senior members of the Nazi regime only, with lower ranking offenders tried in national courts. The ad hoc international tribunals for the former Yugoslavia and Rwanda, based in The Hague and Arusha, Tanzania, respectively, have likewise focused their attention on senior officials, with national courts dealing with subordinates. The Statute of the International Criminal Court, adopted in 1998, foresees that national courts will hear most cases involving international crimes – as British Foreign Minister Jack Straw was at pains to point out following Saddam's arrest. But the ICC statute allows the court to determine whether a fair and genuine prosecution will take place at the national level, and to insist that the case be transferred in the event of domestic failings. Most importantly, the UN Security Council has the legal authority to order that any particular situation involving international crimes be dealt with at the international level.

Saddam Hussein could easily have been tried in a special international court created by the UN Security Council, providing that its veto-holding permanent members agreed. Agreement was achieved with regard to ad hoc tribunals for Yugoslavia, Rwanda and, most recently, Sierra Leone, with considerable dividends in international legitimacy.

The Sierra Leone court is a particularly useful model. A hybrid institution, the court in Freetown includes international judges appointed by the United Nations and local judges appointed by the government of Sierra Leone. A similar court, authorized by both the UN Security Council and the Iraqi Governing Council, would have ensured the highest standards of due process for Saddam's trial. Most importantly, the involvement of the United Nations and judges who are neither Iraqi nor from coalition countries would have guaranteed objectivity, while sending a powerful message that the evils perpetrated under Saddam's regime were crimes against humanity, that his trial and sentence was not simply 'victor's justice', and that the reconstruction of Iraq had become a global responsibility. Simultaneously, an Iraqi-international court would have given the Iraqi people a sense of ownership in the process while remaining global in scope. After twelve long years of UN sanctions, a purely UN process would have been regarded with as much scepticism by Iraqis as a court appointed by the United States. Instead, we have the worst of both worlds: a court run and staffed by Iraqis thirsty for revenge that, behind the scenes, is dependent on – and responsive to – the foreign government that engineered Saddam's downfall for its own ends.

In The Hague, another tough and cagey former dictator is causing difficulties. More than three years into his detention, Slobodan Milošević has outlived his nemesis, the presiding judge in his trial at the International Criminal Tribunal for the former Yugoslavia, Richard May. Milošević has also, through fierce determination and cross-examination, exposed the case against him to be less solid than first appeared. Command responsibility – ordering a crime, or failing to stop a crime that a commander knows or should know is about to occur – is notoriously difficult to prove.

Milošević began his defence in August 2004, after his fragile health had repeatedly delayed the proceedings. With high blood pressure putting him at risk of a heart attack or stroke, Milošević continually demands more time to rest. Court-appointed lawyers were assigned to represent him, but they then asked to be relieved of their duties after he refused to co-operate. In any event, the trial will continue until Milošević is acquitted, convicted or dies. The judges, who are insulated from political pressure by their diverse origins, high salaries and pending retirements, can be expected to show more resilience on this issue than did British Prime Minister Tony Blair and then Home Secretary Jack Straw when dealing with the ageing former Chilean dictator Augusto Pinochet (who they released because of his ostensible dementia, only to have him ruled fit to stand trial in Chile). They might even grant Milošević his rightful wish and call Blair and other NATO leaders – past and present – as witnesses. In principle, this order would have to be obeyed, since the Yugoslav tribunal is a creation of the UN Security Council.

Milošević, who faces charges of crimes against humanity, war crimes and genocide against Bosnian and Kosovar Muslims, claims that he was defending his country against illegal interventions by the United States and NATO. But his allegations of 'victor's justice' ring hollow in a court that was approved by Russia and China, is staffed by lawyers and judges from around the world, and has provided him with seemingly endless opportunities to speak and cross-examine witnesses. It is difficult to imagine the authorities in Belgrade conducting a similarly unbiased prosecution, or one that so carefully protects Milošević's right to a full and rigorous defence.

Moreover, Slobodan Milošević's alleged crimes are international in scope. Bosnia-Herzegovina and Croatia were independent countries during part of the conflict, and the allegations against Milošević are crimes under international law. International criminal courts are needed most when the objectivity of a purely national process would be suspect, and there is an international dimension to the crimes themselves. International courts can be remarkably fair. In 2004, the Special Court for Sierra Leone ruled that its president, Geoffrey Robertson QC, could not participate in cases concerning the Sierra Leone rebels because of condemnations he had published prior to becoming a judge. It is difficult to imagine the Iraqi special tribunal taking similar steps to ensure the appearance and reality of objectivity. The problem with the Milošević trial is not the considerable time it has taken or the grandstanding opportunities provided for the accused, but rather that we are simply not accustomed to seeing former heads of state being prosecuted – and prosecuted properly at that.

Take Ariel Sharon, for example. There is no shortage of allegations against the current Israeli prime minister and former army officer, starting with the 1953 massacre of sixty-nine civilians in the Jordanian village of Qibya, the 1982 slaughter of a thousand Palestinians in the Lebanese refugee camps of Sabra and Shatila, and, in 2004, the 'targeted killings' of the Hamas leaders Sheikh Ahmad Yassin and Abdel-Aziz al-Rantissi. Even the ever-cautious Jack Straw, now the British Foreign Secretary, described the latter acts as 'unlawful'.

Nor is there any shortage of law. In 1951, Israel ratified all four of the 1949 Geneva Conventions. The Israeli government, aware that many of its actions are inconsistent with the Conventions, argues that they do not apply to the Occupied Territories because there was no prior sovereign. But this hair-splitting argument does not circumvent the now accepted status of the Geneva Conventions as customary international law, or the fact that some of the allegations against Sharon concern crimes in Jordan and Lebanon.

The challenges in the case of Sharon, and many others, concern issues of custody, immunity and jurisdiction. Many legal systems require accused individuals to be physically present at their trials. Sharon keeps well clear of countries where he might be arrested and any country that dared to detain him would likely have to reckon with the Israeli Defence Force. Even trials in absentia can be subject to political pressure. In Brussels, an investigative judge had to abandon an attempt to try Sharon in 2003 after the Belgian government succumbed to Israeli and US pressure to modify the legislation under which the prosecution was taking place.

As long as Sharon remains prime minister of Israel, he benefits from immunity from arrest and prosecution under customary international law. In the Pinochet case, the House of Lords held that this immunity does not extend to former heads of state for certain types of crimes. But in a case arising out of the Belgian legislation (before the law was altered) the International Court of Justice held that current heads of state and ministers remain immune. Slobodan Milošević has no immunity before the Yugoslav tribunal because the UN Security Council removed that protection, while the statute of the International Criminal Court similarly states that immunities do not apply. The United States would veto any attempt to use the Security Council against Israel, and Israel will not ratify the statute of the ICC.

Under the principle of universal jurisdiction, any country may prosecute war crimes and crimes against humanity committed by anyone anywhere. For example, Adolf Eichmann, the architect of Hitler's 'final solution', was abducted from Argentina and tried and executed in Israel in 1962 for crimes he committed in Europe during the Second World War. Jurisdiction can also vest on the basis of the crime being committed on a country's territory or the perpetrator being a national of the prosecuting state. In some instances, jurisdiction will also exist if the victims are nationals of the prosecuting state or the crime poses a security threat to that state. Custody, immunity and jurisdiction do not pose impediments to the trial of Saddam Hussein by a national court in Baghdad.

When international courts and tribunals are created, stricter jurisdictional limits are usually imposed. The Yugoslav tribunal has jurisdiction over all war crimes and crimes against humanity committed in the former Yugoslavia since 1991. The jurisdiction of the Rwanda tribunal is limited to crimes committed in 1994. The International Criminal Court has jurisdiction over crimes committed after 1 July 2002, but only if they were committed on the territory, or by the nationals, of ratifying countries. The International Court of Justice – which like the Yugoslav tribunal and ICC sits in The Hague – is only able to hear disputes between nation-states that consent to its jurisdiction; it cannot prosecute individuals. However, when asked to do so by the UN General Assembly, the ICJ may issue an 'advisory opinion' – a non-binding answer to a specific question of law – even if the matter concerns the behaviour of a non-consenting country.

In July 2004, for example, the International Court of Justice advised that the so-called 'security fence' being constructed around and through the West Bank was incompatible with the Geneva Conventions and customary international law. Although the decision is a public relations blow to the Israeli government, the advisory opinion is a far cry from a criminal indictment of Sharon. Any prosecution of the Israeli prime minister will have to wait until he retires or is removed from office and travels to a country that is courageous and principled enough to place him under arrest.

The fact is that most alleged war criminals will never appear in the dock. The few that do are those who have lost political power and the protection of powerful friends, which gives rise to the accusation that international criminal law is simply 'victor's justice'. It is in this context that the International Criminal Court provides something dramatically new: a permanent court, largely immune to political interference, which can take over when countries are unable or unwilling to try alleged perpetrators, and to which the UN Security Council can assign jurisdiction over situations rather than having to create new tribunals each time from scratch. Although the ICC has yet to hear its first case, an investigation is under way, at the request of the Ugandan government, into atrocities committed by the Lord's Resistance Army in northern Uganda.

Close to half of the world's countries have ratified the ICC statute, including all the members of the European Union, Canada, Australia and over one quarter of African states. Only the United States has actively endeavoured to undermine the court. With troops in more than 140 countries, a propensity to intervene under dubious legal circumstances, and interpretations of the laws of war that sometimes differ from those of other states, the single superpower feels vulnerable to international mechanisms for enforcing international criminal law. Whereas the Clinton Administration sought to negotiate protections against the abuse of international procedures into the statutes of the tribunals it helped to create, the Bush Administration has adopted an entirely hostile stance. The US position could not consistently accommodate the use of an international tribunal to try Saddam and is uncomfortable with the Yugoslav and Rwanda tribunals.

Since coming to office, President Bush has 'un-signed' the ICC statute, pressured the UN Security Council into temporarily exempting US forces from the Court's jurisdiction, and obtained more than ninety bilateral treaties committing individual countries not to surrender US citizens to The Hague. Bush has even signed legislation that authorizes him to use military force to secure the release of any US service member detained by the ICC. The law is popularly known as 'The Hague Invasion Act'.

For the last six years, most international lawyers have insisted that the United States has nothing to fear from the ICC, because the Court cannot act if countries' own courts are willing and able to prosecute. But this assumes that alleged crimes will always be investigated diligently and prosecuted by US military lawyers, which might not occur if orders to commit the crimes (or policies encouraging them) originate at the highest levels. The torture at Abu Ghraib prison in Iraq – together with the subsequently leaked memorandum that sought to justify all but the most extreme methods of interrogation – certainly call the assumption of US prosecutorial diligence into question. Had Saddam ratified the ICC statute, the chief prosecutor would, quite properly, already be investigating the Abu Ghraib situation, with a view to possibly laying charges for command responsibility against the secretary of defense and president.

The United States, with British support, sought to protect itself against this kind of risk. UN Security Council Resolution 1422, adopted on 12 June 2002, provided immunity from ICC jurisdiction to the personnel of any non-party to the Court engaged in

UN-authorized action. Although initially intended to protect US soldiers active in UN peacekeeping, the resolution arguably also provided protection for US soldiers and their superiors in Iraq – if one accepts the controversial argument advanced by the US and Britain that the war was, in fact, implicitly authorized by the United Nations.

Although Resolution 1422 originally provided only twelve months of immunity, it was subsequently renewed. The resolution seemed destined to be renewed again in June 2004, until the Abu Ghraib prison scandal broke. Faced with an unexpected wave of opposition to any notion of US military immunity, the United States withdrew the draft resolution that would have provided another extension. The immunity lapsed. In practical legal terms, this may have little effect, given the more than ninety bilateral treaties that commit other countries not to surrender US nationals to the ICC. In political terms, the opposition to the extension of the US immunity was hugely significant because it showed that many countries had finally lost patience with the Bush Administration's contemptuous attitude toward international law. Saddam Hussein's show trial in Baghdad will only exacerbate the tension between a world that still wants a fair and sustainable international legal system and a single superpower that hardly seems to care.

Epilogue

War Law and the Single Superpower

In the early 1940s, German soldiers shaved off the beards of Orthodox Jews. In January 2002, US soldiers did the same to Islamic fundamentalists captured in Afghanistan, before flying them to a detention centre at the US naval base in Guantánamo Bay, Cuba. Given the religious significance that some devout Muslims attach to their beards, the action, which the Pentagon sought to justify on hygienic grounds, probably violated the detainees' right to human dignity under the Third Geneva Convention, several international human rights treaties and customary international law. At best, it was patently insensitive and unnecessary.

Other aspects of the United States' immediate response to the terrorist attacks of 11 September 2001 were similarly troubling. During the Afghan War, hundreds of civilians were killed or maimed as a result of careless targeting; thousands more were put at risk by unexploded cluster bomblets. At Mazar-i-Sharif, fifty detainees died with their hands tied behind their backs when air-to-surface missiles were used to suppress a prison revolt. The destruction of the Al-Jazeera television bureau in Kabul, plans for special military commissions with relaxed evidentiary standards, and the refusal to presume that detainees were prisoners of war all indicated at best a casual – and at worst a maniacal – disregard for international opinion and, more importantly, international humanitarian law. Most disturbing, however, were some of the threats uttered by President George W. Bush. The assertion that 'you're either with us or against us' obviated a central aspect of state sovereignty – the right not to be involved – and recast the

United States as the ultimate arbiter of right and wrong. The identification of an 'axis of evil' between Iran, Iraq and North Korea, and the concurrent claim to a greatly extended right of pre-emptive self-defence, challenged one of the twentieth century's greatest achievements: the prohibition of the threat or use of force in international affairs. Although it was possible at the time to think that the aberration was temporary, it is now clear – particularly after Bush's re-election in November 2004 – that something fundamental has changed.

The United States wields more power than any political entity since the Roman Empire. With twelve aircraft carriers and their accompanying task forces ranging the world's oceans, the only significant heavy airlift capacity and the only major stocks of precision-guided missiles and bombs, the US military can defeat any opponent with only minimal losses. And thanks to its massive defence budget, the United States is the only country that regularly makes major advances in military technology. Simultaneously, decisions reached in Washington and on Wall Street reverberate around the world. Corporate America, the regulatory infrastructure that supports it and the pension funds that propel it, are the dominant influences on economic policy in Latin America, Africa, Asia and even Europe, not to mention on the World Bank, the International Monetary Fund and the World Trade Organization. The 2001 collapse of Enron demonstrated the fragility of US corporate structures, but it also exposed the fevered mating that goes on between business and political elites. Until its demise, Enron was more influential than all but a handful of nation-states. A couple of years ago, I asked an Argentine diplomat what he thought about his country becoming part of the Free Trade Area of the Americas, then being negotiated at the initiative of a number of US-based corporations. He replied, with heavy regret: 'We have no choice.'

A country as powerful as the United States has many choices, even when struck by a blow as heavy as that delivered on 11 September 2001. George W. Bush notwithstanding, Dick Cheney,

Condoleezza Rice and Donald Rumsfeld were quick to spot the opportunities presented by the crisis. Doubters need only think of Jo Moore, adviser to Stephen Byers, the former British Transport Minister, who got into trouble for suggesting that the attack on the World Trade Center provided a perfect opportunity to bury bad news. The battle-hardened ideologues directing US foreign policy are no less cynical, and considerably more adept.

A 'coalition' was constructed to facilitate the freezing of terrorist assets and the gathering of intelligence overseas. But America's allies were fooling themselves to think that the events of 11 September had persuaded the Bush Administration of the value of multilateralism. On the contrary, the mistreatment of detainees at Guantánamo Bay and elsewhere, the renewed threatening of 'rogue states' and the 2003 invasion of Iraq have demonstrated renewed commitment to a unilateralist course.

During its first eight months in office, in 2001, the Bush Administration publicly rejected the Anti-Ballistic Missile Treaty, the Kyoto Protocol on global warming, the Rome Statute of the International Criminal Court, a convention on the sale and transfer of small arms and a protocol to the Biological Weapons Convention. Following 11 September, the United States rejected offers of a UN Security Council resolution to authorize the Afghan War, instead relying on an extended claim of self-defence against state sponsors of terrorism. The United States forged new alliances with illiberal regimes in Pakistan, Kyrgyzstan, Tajikistan and Uzbekistan, reversing years of efforts to promote human rights. And the US advanced a new, greatly extended conception of pre-emptive self-defence, setting in course the invasion of Iraq. In an age of increasing interdependence and cooperation, President Bush and his advisers were deliberately out of step with most of the Western world.

In many respects, Bush's team was a reincarnation of the second Reagan Administration, which was also stridently unilateralist; it, too, drew explicit distinctions between good and evil, claimed exceptional rights, promoted missile defence (and thus a new arms race extending into space) and relied on the threat of terrorism to justify it all. Following the terrorist bombing in 1986 of a Berlin discotheque frequented by US servicemen, then Secretary of State George Shultz said it was 'absurd to argue that international law prohibits us from capturing terrorists in international waters or airspace; from attacking them on the soil of other nations, even for the purpose of rescuing hostages; or from using force against states that support, train and harbour terrorists or guerrillas'. George W. Bush's speechwriter could not have put it better, but there were two important differences between the situations in 1986 and 2001. The end of the Cold War transformed the United States into an unrivalled superpower, making it more likely that claims to use force unilaterally would meet with acquiescence on the part of other countries. More important, the events of 11 September transformed a traditionally isolationist population into a nation that wanted its president to act decisively on the world stage. Despite obvious setbacks, much of the American populace retains this desire. It is likely to continue to do so, given that the 'war on terrorism' has been linked by Bush's advisers to three strands of thought that are central to the way Americans think about themselves.

The first is a narrow, reactionary conception of popular sovereignty. The US Constitution is regarded as the ultimate expression of the American people's consent to be governed; any exercise of authority not expressly vested in the Constitution is considered illegitimate. International law, which necessarily results from the joint law-making efforts of numerous countries, immediately attracts suspicion, particularly from the Republican Right. The suspicion is heightened by the possibility that international law might provide the means for the Federal Government of the United States – whose constitutional powers in the field of foreign relations are considerable – to override the careful delimitation between its powers and those of the fifty 'States of the Union'. Concern on the part of the Right about the aggrandizement of federal powers on the back of international law is most acute with regard to police and criminal justice matters, where the Constitution accords primary responsibility to the states.

This anxiety about popular sovereignty helps explain why, during the negotiation of the UN Charter in 1945, the United States insisted on a veto over Security Council resolutions. Anything less would have violated the US Constitution. In 2001, US negotiators sabotaged a treaty designed to regulate the international trade in light weapons, on the basis that it would violate the constitutional right to bear arms. At the same time, President Bush dismissed international concern over the execution of juvenile and mentally handicapped offenders in the United States as impermissible interference in domestic affairs. In terms of its adherence to a seventeenth-century, absolutist conception of sovereignty, the United States ranks with Burma, China, Iran and North Korea.

The second strand of thought influencing US foreign policy draws on Frederick Jackson Turner's 'frontier thesis', according to which the uniquely individualistic and entrepreneurial character of American society derives from the historical ability of its people to escape government control by moving to the frontier. Much of the history of US foreign policy could be explained as an ongoing attempt to acquire new frontiers. The United States spent much of its first century conquering or buying vast tracts of land from France, Russia, Mexico and the Indian tribes. The world outside North America was of little interest, except when it threatened the United States. The articulation of the Monroe Doctrine in 1823 suggested broader ambitions by signalling that the United States would not tolerate interventions in the Western hemisphere on the part of the Holy Alliance (a reactionary grouping of Austria, Prussia and Russia, agreed by their monarchs in 1815). By the end of the nineteenth century, the United States had turned its attention abroad. Its seizure of Cuba in 1898 contributed to the outbreak of the Spanish-American War, which gave the United States control of Hawaii, the Philippines and the Panama Canal Zone. The First World War brought a close alliance with Britain, which enabled the United States to join in that country's domination of international politics until the end of the Second World War. By then, America was alone at the top, with the Soviet Union emerging as the second great power. Forty years of nuclear rivalry and proxy wars fostered an imperialist vision, a powerful military-industrial complex and the extension of US influence around the globe.

The collapse of the Soviet Union marked the end of an epoch, but not the end of US involvement in the rest of the world. Other countries had become the 'new frontier' and the heads of US-based corporations the new frontiersmen. The focus of government policy shifted to making the world a more hospitable place for American business. The creation of the World Trade Organization – an institution grounded in the free-market assumptions of the 'Washington Consensus' (a collection of neo-liberal policies imposed by the World Bank and International Monetary Fund on developing countries after the Cold War) – was a notable achievement in this regard. The opening up of Iraq to Halliburton (Vice President Dick Cheney's former company) and other US-based multinationals may well have been another.

The frontier thesis lives on in everyday life too. The stereotypical middle-class American is a hardworking, gun-owning 'handyman', who lives in a large wooden house in a far-flung suburb and drives a four-ton SUV. After 11 September, President Bush's use of such expressions as 'dead or alive', 'let's roll', and 'smoking out of holes' resonated in the United States, helping him achieve dizzying heights in the polls; in November 2004, it helped him win re-election.

The third strand of thought concerns the faith that Americans have in technology. Technology is the ultimate panacea, whether for cancer, hyperactive children, climate change or terrorism. Even the almost invisible teleprompter that enables George W. Bush to deliver flawless speeches – looking straight through it at his audience – is celebrated as a technological achievement. In October 2004, most Americans were unconcerned by the possibility that the president was being coached through an earpiece during the election debates.

Technological superiority is a central theme of the one author we can be sure George W. Bush has read. In Tom Clancy's 2001 novel *The Bear and the Dragon*, technology enables the United States to follow the inner deliberations of the Chinese government, rout the Chinese army and ward off an intercontinental ballistic missile attack. Most of the Bush Administration's foreign policy up to 11 September was prefigured by Clancy, including missile defence, closer and closer links with Russia, reliance on the dutiful cooperation of Tony Blair, and a general lack of concern for the Chinese – referred to as 'Klingons' by Clancy's fictional Republican presidential hero. (Bush presumably also read Clancy's 1996 book, *Debt of Honor*, in which terrorists seize control of a jumbo jet and crash it into the Capitol Building, killing the president, Supreme Court and most of the Congress, though this story apparently had less impact on him.) Today, with their faith in technology reaffirmed by the apparent effectiveness of precision-guided missiles and bombs in the Afghan and Iraq Wars, many Americans are more than willing to see increased spending on high-tech weapons.

Powerful countries have always shaped the international system to their advantage. In the sixteenth century, Spain redefined basic concepts of justice and universality to justify the conquest of indigenous Americans. In the eighteenth century, France developed the modern concepts of borders and the 'balance of power' to suit its continental strengths. In the nineteenth century, Britain introduced new rules on piracy, neutrality and colonialism, again to suit its interests as the predominant power of the day.

George W. Bush's United States has been no different, except that, following 11 September 2001, hardly anyone was prepared to challenge its lead. The President's advisers took full advantage of the situation, applying pressure in pursuit of numerous goals that, under normal circumstances, could not have been achieved. Prominent among these goals has been greater flexibility to use force outside the UN Charter (through the extension of the right of self-defence to include action against state sponsors of terrorism and a much elongated right of pre-emptive action) as well as with regard to targeting and the treatment of detainees. To the degree that it succeeds in these law-changing initiatives – and it has not yet succeeded with the pre-emption, targeting and treatment claims – the United States contributes to marginalizing the United Nations in international peace and security, an area over which the Security Council was assigned 'primary responsibility' in 1945, and to diminishing fundamental human protections. By marginalizing the United Nations, it makes it more difficult for governments to draw upon this important source of legitimacy for the use of military force across borders. By undermining international humanitarian law, it squanders moral authority and the capacity to persuade and influence others. All this in turn diminishes the potential for cooperative, multilateral responses to threats and breaches of the peace, responses that would share the military and financial burdens of intervention among larger groups of countries and reduce the resentments that armed interventions so easily feed.

The actions of the United States have also made it more difficult to criticize violations of international law by other countries, most notably Israel. The use by the CIA of a Predator drone to kill six terrorist suspects in northern Yemen in November 2002 is difficult to distinguish from 'targeted killings', and the storm-trooper tactics of US soldiers in post-war Iraq are explicitly modelled on those of the Israeli Defence Force. The testimonies of Palestinians released from Israeli prisons – as well as those of six Britons released from Saudi Arabia in 2003 – bear more than a passing resemblance to the photographs taken at Abu Ghraib prison, and the stories told by detainees released from Bagram airbase and Guantánamo Bay.

Terrorism can cause great destruction and upheaval, but efforts to stamp it out can serve as a smokescreen for the pursuit of less worthy goals. America's friends and allies, while providing strong support for the American people, should offer their cooperation on specific issues only after careful consideration of their best interests, which prominently include the maintenance of a just, strong, equal and effective system of international law. Even if the United States has abdicated its leadership role in the struggle for a global system of justice and human rights, its partners in that effort must continue the fight.

There is regularly talk of a 'democratic deficit' with regard to supranational institutions such as the United Nations, World Trade Organization and European Union, whereby important decisions are made without there being much accountability to most of the people affected. Perhaps it is time to start speaking of a similar deficit with regard to the United States. Decisions made in Washington today eclipse the importance of decisions made in the United Nations – and not just for Americans. Citizens of other countries consequently find themselves in a position full of irony. Subject to the governance of a foreign power but deprived of any voice, the people of the world have become the victims of a twenty-first-century form of 'taxation without representation' – the very grievance that sparked the American Revolution of 1776.

Although imperfect, the international rules and institutions detested by neo-conservatives such as George W. Bush are more consistent with the founding principles of the United States than the imperialist principles to which they now subscribe. The Declaration of Independence affirms that the representatives of the United States will have a 'due regard for the opinions of other nations'. Many Americans maintain a strong desire to see their country return to the constructive, cooperative, law-abiding approach that led to the creation of the United Nations in 1945 at a conference in San Francisco. It's high time that America's friends supported them, by resolutely opposing the rule-twisting megalomaniacs who have dominated and corrupted US and global politics since 11 September 2001. The immense power of the United States carries with it an awesome responsibility: to improve the world – for everyone. Obeying the requirements of war law is a necessary first step.

Appendix

Charter of the United Nations, 1945

Preamble

We the Peoples of the United Nations Determined

to save succeeding generations from the scourge of war, which twice in our lifetime has brought untold sorrow to mankind, and

to reaffirm faith in fundamental human rights, in the dignity and worth of the human person, in the equal rights of men and women and of nations large and small, and

to establish conditions under which justice and respect for the obligations arising from treaties and other sources of international law can be maintained, and

to promote social progress and better standards of life in larger freedom,

And for these Ends

to practice tolerance and live together in peace with one another as good neighbors, and

to unite our strength to maintain international peace and security, and

to ensure by the acceptance of principles and the institution of methods, that armed force shall not be used, save in the common interest, and

to employ international machinery for the promotion of the economic and social advancement of all peoples,

Have Resolved to Combine our Efforts to Accomplish these Aims

Accordingly, our respective Governments, through representatives assembled in the city of San Francisco, who have exhibited their full powers found to be in good and due form, have agreed to the present Charter of the United Nations and do hereby establish an international organization to be known as the United Nations.

Chapter I
Purposes and Principles
Article 1

The Purposes of the United Nations are:

1. To maintain international peace and security, and to that end: to take effective collective measures for the prevention and removal of threats to the peace, and for the suppression of acts of aggression or other breaches of the peace, and to bring about by peaceful means, and in conformity with the principles of justice and international law, adjustment or settlement of international disputes or situations which might lead to a breach of the peace;

2. To develop friendly relations among nations based on respect for the principle of equal rights and self-determination of peoples, and to take other appropriate measures to strengthen universal peace;

3. To achieve international cooperation in solving international problems of an economic, social, cultural, or humanitarian character, and in promoting and encouraging respect for human rights and for fundamental freedoms for all without distinction as to race, sex, language, or religion; and

4. To be a center for harmonizing the actions of nations in the attainment of these common ends.

Article 2

The Organization and its Members, in pursuit of the Purposes stated in Article 1, shall act in accordance with the following Principles.

1. The Organization is based on the principle of the sovereign equality of all its Members.

2. All Members, in order to ensure to all of them the rights and benefits resulting from membership, shall fulfill in good faith the obligations assumed by them in accordance with the present Charter.

3. All Members shall settle their international disputes by peaceful means in such a manner that international peace and security, and justice, are not endangered.

4. All Members shall refrain in their international relations from the threat or use of force against the territorial integrity or political independence of any state, or in any other manner inconsistent with the Purposes of the United Nations.

5. All Members shall give the United Nations every assistance in any action it takes in accordance with the present Charter, and shall refrain

from giving assistance to any state against which the United Nations is taking preventive or enforcement action.

6. The Organization shall ensure that states which are not Members of the United Nations act in accordance with these Principles so far as may be necessary for the maintenance of international peace and security.

7. Nothing contained in the present Charter shall authorize the United Nations to intervene in matters which are essentially within the domestic jurisdiction of any state or shall require the Members to submit such matters to settlement under the present Charter; but this principle shall not prejudice the application of enforcement measures under Chapter VII.

Chapter II
Membership

Article 3

The original Members of the United Nations shall be the states which, having participated in the United Nations Conference on International Organization at San Francisco, or having previously signed the Declaration by United Nations of January 1, 1942, sign the present Charter and ratify it in accordance with Article 110.

Article 4

1. Membership in the United Nations is open to all other peace-loving states which accept the obligations contained in the present Charter and, in the judgment of the Organization, are able and willing to carry out these obligations.

2. The admission of any such state to membership in the United Nations will be effected by a decision of the General Assembly upon the recommendation of the Security Council.

Article 5

A member of the United Nations against which preventive or enforcement action has been taken by the Security Council may be suspended from the exercise of the rights and privileges of membership by the General Assembly upon the recommendation of the Security Council. The exercise of these rights and privileges may be restored by the Security Council.

Article 6

A Member of the United Nations which has persistently violated the Principles contained in the present Charter may be expelled from the

Organization by the General Assembly upon the recommendation of the Security Council.

Chapter III
Organs

Article 7

1. There are established as the principal organs of the United Nations: a General Assembly, a Security Council, an Economic and Social Council, a Trusteeship Council, an International Court of Justice, and a Secretariat. 2. Such subsidiary organs as may be found necessary may be established in accordance with the present Charter.

Article 8

The United Nations shall place no restrictions on the eligibility of men and women to participate in any capacity and under conditions of equality in its principal and subsidiary organs.

Chapter IV
The General Assembly
Composition

Article 9

1. The General Assembly shall consist of all the Members of the United Nations. 2. Each member shall have not more than five representatives in the General Assembly.

Functions and Powers

Article 10

The General Assembly may discuss any questions or any matters within the scope of the present Charter or relating to the powers and functions of any organs provided for in the present Charter, and, except as provided in Article 12, may make recommendations to the Members of the United Nations or to the Security Council or to both on any such questions or matters.

Article 11

1. The General Assembly may consider the general principles of coopera-tion in the maintenance of international peace and security, including the principles governing disarmament and the regulation of armaments, and may make recommendations with regard to such principles to the Members or to the Security Council or to both.

2. The General Assembly may discuss any questions relating to the main-tenance of international peace and security brought before it by any Member of the United Nations, or by the Security Council, or by a state which is not a Member of the United Nations in accordance with Article 35, paragraph 2, and, except as provided in Article 12, may make recom-mendations with regard to any such questions to the state or states concerned or to the Security Council or to both. Any such question on which action is necessary shall be referred to the Security Council by the General Assembly either before or after discussion.

3. The General Assembly may call the attention of the Security Council to situations which are likely to endanger international peace and security.

4. The powers of the General Assembly set forth in this Article shall not limit the general scope of Article 10.

Article 12

1. While the Security Council is exercising in respect of any dispute or situation the functions assigned to it in the present Charter, the General Assembly shall not make any recommendation with regard to that dispute or situation unless the Security Council so requests.

2. The Secretary-General, with the consent of the Security Council, shall notify the General Assembly at each session of any matters relative to the maintenance of international peace and security which are being dealt with by the Security Council and shall similarly notify the General Assembly, or the Members of the United Nations if the General Assembly is not in session, immediately the Security Council ceases to deal with such matters.

Article 13

1. The General Assembly shall initiate studies and make recommenda-tions for the purpose of:

a. promoting international cooperation in the political field and encouraging the progressive development of international law and its codification;

b. promoting international cooperation in the economic, social, cultural, educational, and health fields, and assisting in the realization of human rights and fundamental freedoms for all without distinction as to race, sex, language, or religion.

2. The further responsibilities, functions and powers of the General Assembly with respect to matters mentioned in paragraph 1(b) above are set forth in Chapters IX and X.

Article 14

Subject to the provisions of Article 12, the General Assembly may recommend measures for the peaceful adjustment of any situation, regardless of origin, which it deems likely to impair the general welfare or friendly relations among nations, including situations resulting from a violation of the provisions of the present Charter setting forth the Purposes and Principles of the United Nations.

Article 15

1. The General Assembly shall receive and consider annual and special reports from the Security Council; these reports shall include an account of the measures that the Security Council has decided upon or taken to maintain international peace and security.

2. The General Assembly shall receive and consider reports from the other organs of the United Nations.

Article 16

The General Assembly shall perform such functions with respect to the international trusteeship system as are assigned to it under Chapters XII and XIII, including the approval of the trusteeship agreements for areas not designated as strategic.

Article 17

1. The General Assembly shall consider and approve the budget of the Organization.

2. The expenses of the Organization shall be borne by the Members as apportioned by the General Assembly.

3. The General Assembly shall consider and approve any financial and budgetary arrangements with specialized agencies referred to in Article 57 and shall examine the administrative budgets of such specialized agencies with a view to making recommendations to the agencies concerned.

Voting

Article 18

1. Each member of the General Assembly shall have one vote.

2. Decisions of the General Assembly on important questions shall be made by a two-thirds majority of the members present and voting. These questions shall include: recommendations with respect to the maintenance of international peace and security, the election of the non-permanent members of the Security Council, the election of the members of the Economic and Social Council, the election of members of the Trusteeship Council in accordance with paragraph 1(c) of Article 86, the admission of new Members to the United Nations, the suspension of the rights and privileges of membership, the expulsion of Members, questions relating to the operation of the trusteeship system, and budgetary questions.

3. Decisions on other questions, Composition including the determination of additional categories of questions to be decided by a two-thirds majority, shall be made by a majority of the members present and voting.

Article 19

A Member of the United Nations which is in arrears in the payment of its financial contributions to the Organization shall have no vote in the General Assembly if the amount of its arrears equals or exceeds the amount of the contributions due from it for the preceding two full years. The General Assembly may, nevertheless, permit such a Member to vote if it is satisfied that the failure to pay is due to conditions beyond the control of the Member.

Procedure

Article 20

The General Assembly shall meet in regular annual sessions and in such special sessions as occasion may require. Special sessions shall be convoked by the Secretary-General at the request of the Security Council or of a majority of the Members of the United Nations.

Article 21

The General Assembly shall adopt its own rules of procedure. It shall elect its President for each session.

Article 22

The General Assembly may establish such subsidiary organs as it deems necessary for the performance of its functions.

Chapter V
The Security Council

Article 23

1. The Security Council shall consist of fifteen Members of the United Nations. The Republic of China, France, the Union of Soviet Socialist Republics, the United Kingdom of Great Britain and Northern Ireland, and the United States of America shall be permanent members of the Security Council. The General Assembly shall elect ten other Members of the United Nations to be non-permanent members of the Security Council, due regard being specially paid, in the first instance to the contribution of Members of the United Nations to the maintenance of international peace and security and to the other purposes of the Organization, and also to equitable geographical distribution.
2. The non-permanent members of the Security Council shall be elected for a term of two years. In the first election of the non-permanent members after the increase of the membership of the Security Council from eleven to fifteen, two of the four additional members shall be chosen for a term of one year. A retiring member shall not be eligible for immediate re-election.
3. Each member of the Security Council shall have one representative.

Functions and Powers

Article 24

1. In order to ensure prompt and effective action by the United Nations, its Members confer on the Security Council primary responsibility for the maintenance of international peace and security, and agree that in carrying out its duties under this responsibility the Security Council acts on their behalf.
2. In discharging these duties the Security Council shall act in accordance with the Purposes and Principles of the United Nations. The specific powers granted to the Security Council for the discharge of these duties are laid down in Chapters VI, VII, VIII, and XII.
3. The Security Council shall submit annual and, when necessary, special reports to the General Assembly for its consideration.

Article 25

The Members of the United Nations agree to accept and carry out the decisions of the Security Council in accordance with the present Charter.

Article 26

In order to promote the establishment and maintenance of international peace and security with the least diversion for armaments of the world's human and economic resources, the Security Council shall be responsible for formulating, with the assistance of the Military Staff Committee referred to in Article 47, plans to be submitted to the Members of the United Nations for the establishment of a system for the regulation of armaments.

Voting

Article 27

1. Each member of the Security Council shall have one vote.
2. Decisions of the Security Council on procedural matters shall be made by an affirmative vote of nine members.
3. Decisions of the Security Council on all other matters shall be made by an affirmative vote of nine members including the concurring votes of the permanent members; provided that, in decisions under Chapter VI, and under paragraph 3 of Article 52, a party to a dispute shall abstain from voting.

Procedure

Article 28

1. The Security Council shall be so organized as to be able to function continuously. Each member of the Security Council shall for this purpose be represented at all times at the seat of the Organization.
2. The Security Council shall hold periodic meetings at which each of its members may, if it so desires, be represented by a member of the government or by some other specially designated representative.
3. The Security Council may hold meetings at such places other than the seat of the Organization as in its judgment will best facilitate its work.

Article 29

The Security Council may establish such subsidiary organs as it deems necessary for the performance of its functions.

Article 30

The Security Council shall adopt its own rules of procedure, including the method of selecting its President.

Article 31

Any Member of the United Nations which is not a member of the Security Council may participate, without vote, in the discussion of any question brought before the Security Council whenever the latter considers that the interests of that Member are specially affected.

Article 32

Any Member of the United Nations which is not a member of the Security Council or any state which is not a Member of the United Nations, if it is a party to a dispute under consideration by the Security Council, shall be invited to participate, without vote, in the discussion relating to the dispute. The Security Council shall lay down such conditions as it deems just for the participation of a state which is not a Member of the United Nations.

Chapter VI
Pacific Settlement of Disputes

Article 33

1. The parties to any dispute, the continuance of which is likely to endanger the maintenance of international peace and security, shall, first of all, seek a solution by negotiation, enquiry, mediation, conciliation, arbitration, judicial settlement, resort to regional agencies or arrangements, or other peaceful means of their own choice.
2. The Security Council shall, when it deems necessary, call upon the parties to settle their dispute by such means.

Article 34

The Security Council may investigate any dispute, or any situation which might lead to international friction or give rise to a dispute, in order to determine whether the continuance of the dispute or situation is likely to endanger the maintenance of international peace and security.

Article 35

1. Any Member of the United Nations may bring any dispute, or any situation of the nature referred to in Article 34, to the attention of the Security Council or of the General Assembly.

2. A state which is not a Member of the United Nations may bring to the attention of the Security Council or of the General Assembly any dispute to which it is a party if it accepts in advance, for the purposes of the dispute, the obligations of pacific settlement provided in the present Charter.

3. The proceedings of the General Assembly in respect of matters brought to its attention under this Article will be subject to the provisions of Articles 11 and 12.

Article 36

1. The Security Council may, at any stage of a dispute of the nature referred to in Article 33 or of a situation of like nature, recommend appropriate procedures or methods of adjustment.

2. The Security Council should take into consideration any procedures for the settlement of the dispute which have already been adopted by the parties.

3. In making recommendations under this Article the Security Council should also take into consideration that legal disputes should as a general rule be referred by the parties to the International Court of Justice in accordance with the provisions of the Statute of the Court.

Article 37

1. Should the parties to a dispute of the nature referred to in Article 33 fail to settle it by the means indicated in that Article, they shall refer it to the Security Council.

2. If the Security Council deems that the continuance of the dispute is in fact likely to endanger the maintenance of international peace and security, it shall decide whether to take action under Article 36 or to recommend such terms of settlement as it may consider appropriate.

Article 38

Without prejudice to the provisions of Articles 33 to 37, the Security Council may, if all the parties to any dispute so request, make recommendations to the parties with a view to a pacific settlement of the dispute.

Chapter VII
Action with respect to Threats to the Peace, Breaches of the Peace, and Acts of Aggression

Article 39

The Security Council shall determine the existence of any threat to the peace, breach of the peace, or act of aggression and shall make recommendations, or decide what measures shall be taken in accordance with Articles 41 and 42, to maintain or restore international peace and security.

Article 40

In order to prevent an aggravation of the situation, the Security Council may, before making the recommendations or deciding upon the measures provided for in Article 39, call upon the parties concerned to comply with such provisional measures as it deems necessary or desirable. Such provisional measures shall be without prejudice to the rights, claims, or position of the parties concerned. The Security Council shall duly take account of failure to comply with such provisional measures.

Article 41

The Security Council may decide what measures not involving the use of armed force are to be employed to give effect to its decisions, and it may call upon the Members of the United Nations to apply such measures. These may include complete or partial interruption of economic relations and of rail, sea, air, postal, telegraphic, radio, and other means of communication, and the severance of diplomatic relations.

Article 42

Should the Security Council consider that measures provided for in Article 41 would be inadequate or have proved to be inadequate, it may take such action by air, sea, or land forces as may be necessary to maintain or restore international peace and security. Such action may include demonstrations, blockade, and other operations by air, sea, or land forces of Members of the United Nations.

Article 43

1. All Members of the United Nations, in order to contribute to the maintenance of international peace and security, undertake to make available to the Security Council, on its call and in accordance with a special

agreement or agreements, armed forces, assistance, and facilities, including rights of passage, necessary for the purpose of maintaining international peace and security.

2. Such agreement or agreements shall govern the numbers and types of forces, their degree of readiness and general location, and the nature of the facilities and assistance to be provided.

3. The agreement or agreements shall be negotiated as soon as possible on the initiative of the Security Council. They shall be concluded between the Security Council and Members or between the Security Council and groups of Members and shall be subject to ratification by the signatory states in accordance with their respective constitutional processes.

Article 44

When the Security Council has decided to use force it shall, before calling upon a Member not represented on it to provide armed forces in fulfillment of the obligations assumed under Article 43, invite that Member, if the Member so desires, to participate in the decisions of the Security Council concerning the employment of contingents of that Member's armed forces.

Article 45

In order to enable the United Nations to take urgent military measures Members shall hold immediately available national air-force contingents for combined international enforcement action. The strength and degree of readiness of these contingents and plans for their combined action shall be determined, within the limits laid down in the special agreement or agreements referred to in Article 43, by the Security Council with the assistance of the Military Staff Committee.

Article 46

Plans for the application of armed force shall be made by the Security Council with the assistance of the Military Staff Committee.

Article 47

1. There shall be established a Military Staff Committee to advise and assist the Security Council on all questions relating to the Security Council's military requirements for the maintenance of international peace and security, the employment and command of forces placed at its disposal, the regulation of armaments, and possible disarmament.

2. The Military Staff Committee shall consist of the Chiefs of Staff of the permanent members of the Security Council or their representatives. Any Member of the United Nations not permanently represented on the Committee shall be invited by the Committee to be associated with it when the efficient discharge of the Committee's responsibilities requires the participation of that Member in its work.

3. The Military Staff Committee shall be responsible under the Security Council for the strategic direction of any armed forces placed at the disposal of the Security Council. Questions relating to the command of such forces shall be worked out subsequently.

4. The Military Staff Committee, with the authorization of the Security Council and after consultation with appropriate regional agencies, may establish regional subcommittees.

Article 48

1. The action required to carry out the decisions of the Security Council for the maintenance of international peace and security shall be taken by all the Members of the United Nations or by some of them, as the Security Council may determine.

2. Such decisions shall be carried out by the Members of the United Nations directly and through their action in the appropriate international agencies of which they are members.

Article 49

The Members of the United Nations shall join in affording mutual assistance in carrying out the measures decided upon by the Security Council.

Article 50

If preventive or enforcement measures against any state are taken by the Security Council, any other state, whether a Member of the United Nations or not, which finds itself confronted with special economic problems arising from the carrying out of those measures shall have the right to consult the Security Council with regard to a solution of those problems.

Article 51

Nothing in the present Charter shall impair the inherent right of individual or collective self-defense if an armed attack occurs against a Member of the United Nations, until the Security Council has taken measures necessary to maintain international peace and security. Measures taken by

Members in the exercise of this right of self-defense shall be immediately reported to the Security Council and shall not in any way affect the authority and responsibility of the Security Council under the present Charter to take at any time such action as it deems necessary in order to maintain or restore international peace and security.

Chapter VIII
Regional Arrangements

Article 52

1. Nothing in the present Charter precludes the existence of regional arrangements or agencies for dealing with such matters relating to the maintenance of international peace and security as are appropriate for regional action, provided that such arrangements or agencies and their activities are consistent with the Purposes and Principles of the United Nations.

2. The Members of the United Nations entering into such arrangements or constituting such agencies shall make every effort to achieve pacific settlement of local disputes through such regional arrangements or by such regional agencies before referring them to the Security Council.

3. The Security Council shall encourage the development of pacific settlement of local disputes through such regional arrangements or by such regional agencies either on the initiative of the states concerned or by reference from the Security Council.

4. This Article in no way impairs the application of Articles 34 and 35.

Article 53

1. The Security Council shall, where appropriate, utilize such regional arrangements or agencies for enforcement action under its authority. But no enforcement action shall be taken under regional arrangements or by regional agencies without the authorization of the Security Council, with the exception of measures against any enemy state, as defined in paragraph 2 of this Article, provided for pursuant to Article 107 or in regional arrangements directed against renewal of aggressive policy on the part of any such state, until such time as the Organization may, on request of the Governments concerned, be charged with the responsibility for preventing further aggression by such a state.

2. The term enemy state as used in paragraph 1 of this Article applies to any state which during the Second World War has been an enemy of any signatory of the present Charter.

Article 54

The Security Council shall at all times be kept fully informed of activities undertaken or in contemplation under regional arrangements or by regional agencies for the maintenance of international peace and security.

Chapter IX
International Economic and Social Cooperation

Article 55

With a view to the creation of conditions of stability and well-being which are necessary for peaceful and friendly relations among nations based on respect for the principle of equal rights and self-determination of peoples, the United Nations shall promote:

a. higher standards of living, full employment, and conditions of economic and social progress and development;

b. solutions of international economic, social, health, and related problems; and international cultural and educational co-operation; and

c. universal respect for, and observance of, human rights and fundamental freedoms for all without distinction as to race, sex, language, or religion.

Article 56

All Members pledge themselves to take joint and separate action in cooperation with the Organization for the achievement of the purposes set forth in Article 55.

Article 57

1. The various specialized agencies, established by intergovernmental agreement and having wide international responsibilities, as defined in their basic instruments, in economic, social, cultural, educational, health, and related fields, shall be brought into relationship with the United Nations in accordance with the provisions of Article 63.

2. Such agencies thus brought into relationship with the United Nations are hereinafter referred to as specialized agencies.

Article 58

The Organization shall make recommendations for the coordination of the policies and activities of the specialized agencies.

Article 59

The Organization shall, where appropriate, initiate negotiations among the states concerned for the creation of any new specialized agencies required for the accomplishment of the purposes set forth in Article 55.

Article 60

Responsibility for the discharge of the functions of the Organization set forth in this Chapter shall be vested in the General Assembly and, under the authority of the General Assembly, in the Economic and Social Council, which shall have for this purpose the powers set forth in Chapter X.

Chapter X
The Economic and Social Council
Composition

Article 61

1. The Economic and Social Council shall consist of fifty-four Members of the United Nations elected by the General Assembly.
2. Subject to the provisions of paragraph 3, eighteen members of the Economic and Social Council shall be elected each year for a term of three years. A retiring member shall be eligible for immediate re-election.
3. At the first election after the increase in the membership of the Economic and Social Council from twenty-seven to fifty-four members, in addition to the members elected in place of the nine members whose term of office expires at the end of that year, twenty-seven additional members shall be elected. Of these twenty-seven additional members, the term of office of nine members so elected shall expire at the end of one year, and of nine other members at the end of two years, in accordance with arrangements made by the General Assembly.
4. Each member of the Economic and Social Council shall have one representative.

Functions and Powers

Article 62

1. The Economic and Social Council may make or initiate studies and reports with respect to international economic, social, cultural, educational, health, and related matters and may make recommendations with

respect to any such matters to the General Assembly, to the Members of the United Nations, and to the specialized agencies concerned.

2. It may make recommendations for the purpose of promoting respect for, and observance of, human rights and fundamental freedoms for all.

3. It may prepare draft conventions for submission to the General Assembly, with respect to matters falling within its competence.

4. It may call, in accordance with the rules prescribed by the United Nations, international conferences on matters falling within its competence.

Article 63

1. The Economic and Social Council may enter into agreements with any of the agencies referred to in Article 57, defining the terms on which the agency concerned shall be brought into relationship with the United Nations. Such agreements shall be subject to approval by the General Assembly.

2. It may coordinate the activities of the specialized agencies through consultation with and recommendations to such agencies and through recommendations to the General Assembly and to the Members of the United Nations.

Article 64

1. The Economic and Social Council may take appropriate steps to obtain regular reports from the specialized agencies. It may make arrangements with the Members of the United Nations and with the specialized agencies to obtain reports on the steps taken to give effect to its own recommendations and to recommendations on matters falling within its competence made by the General Assembly.

2. It may communicate its observations on these reports to the General Assembly.

Article 65

The Economic and Social Council may furnish information to the Security Council and shall assist the Security Council upon its request.

Article 66

1. The Economic and Social Council shall perform such functions as fall within its competence in connection with the carrying out of the recommendations of the General Assembly.

2. It may, with the approval of the General Assembly, perform services at the request of Members of the United Nations and at the request of specialized agencies.

3. It shall perform such other functions as are specified elsewhere in the present Charter or as may be assigned to it by the General Assembly.

Article 67

1. Each member of the Economic and Social Council shall have one vote.

2. Decisions of the Economic and Social Council shall be made by a majority of the members present and voting.

Procedure

Article 68

The Economic and Social Council shall set up commissions in economic and social fields and for the promotion of human rights, and such other commissions as may be required for the performance of its functions.

Article 69

The Economic and Social Council shall invite any Member of the United Nations to participate, without vote, in its deliberations on any matter of particular concern to that Member.

Article 70

The Economic and Social Council may make arrangements for representatives of the specialized agencies to participate, without vote, in its deliberations and in those of the commissions established by it, and for its representatives to participate in the deliberations of the specialized agencies.

Article 71

The Economic and Social Council may make suitable arrangements for consultation with non-governmental organizations which are concerned with matters within its competence. Such arrangements may be made with international organizations and, where appropriate, with national organizations after consultation with the Member of the United Nations concerned.

Article 72

1. The Economic and Social Council shall adopt its own rules of procedure, including the method of selecting its President.
2. The Economic and Social Council shall meet as required in accordance with its rules, which shall include provision for the convening of meetings on the request of a majority of its members.

Chapter XI
Declaration regarding Non-Self-Governing Territories
Article 73

Members of the United Nations which have or assume responsibilities for the administration of territories whose peoples have not yet attained a full measure of self-government recognize the principle that the interests of the inhabitants of these territories are paramount, and accept as a sacred trust the obligation to promote to the utmost, within the system of international peace and security established by the present Charter, the well-being of the inhabitants of these territories, and, to this end:

a. to ensure, with due respect for the culture of the peoples concerned, their political, economic, social, and educational advancement, their just treatment, and their protection against abuses;

b. to develop self-government, to take due account of the political aspirations of the peoples, and to assist them in the progressive development of their free political institutions, according to the particular circumstances of each territory and its peoples and their varying stages of advancement;

c. to further international peace and security;

d. to promote constructive measures of development, to encourage research, and to cooperate with one another and, when and where appropriate, with specialized international bodies with a view to the practical achievement of the social, economic, and scientific purposes set forth in this Article; and

e. to transmit regularly to the Secretary-General for information purposes, subject to such limitation as security and constitutional considerations may require, statistical and other information of a technical nature relating to economic, social, and educational conditions in the territories for which they are respectively responsible other than those territories to which Chapter XII and XIII apply.

Article 74

Members of the United Nations also agree that their policy in respect of the territories to which this Chapter applies, no less than in respect of their metropolitan areas, must be based on the general principle of good-neighborliness, due account being taken of the interests and well-being of the rest of the world, in social, economic, and commercial matters.

Chapter XII
International Trusteeship System

Article 75

The United Nations shall establish under its authority an international trusteeship system for the administration and supervision of such territories as may be placed thereunder by subsequent individual agreements. These territories are hereinafter referred to as trust territories.

Article 76

The basic objectives of the trusteeship system, in accordance with the Purposes of the United Nations laid down in Article 1 of the present Charter, shall be:

a. to further international peace and security;

b. to promote the political, economic, social, and educational advancement of the inhabitants of the trust territories, and their progressive development towards self-government or independence as may be appropriate to the particular circumstances of each territory and its peoples and the freely expressed wishes of the peoples concerned, and as may be provided by the terms of each trusteeship agreement;

c. to encourage respect for human rights and for fundamental freedoms for all without distinction as to race, sex, language, or religion, and to encourage recognition of the interdependence of the peoples of the world; and

d. to ensure equal treatment in social, economic, and commercial matters for all Members of the United Nations and their nationals and also equal treatment for the latter in the administration of justice without prejudice to the attainment of the foregoing objectives and subject to the provisions of Article 80.

Article 77

1. The trusteeship system shall apply to such territories in the following categories as may be placed thereunder by means of trusteeship agreements:

a. territories now held under mandate;

b. territories which may be detached from enemy states as a result of the Second World War, and

c. territories voluntarily placed under the system by states responsible for their administration.

2. It will be a matter for subsequent agreement as to which territories in the foregoing categories will be brought under the trusteeship system and upon what terms.

Article 78

The trusteeship system shall not apply to territories which have become Members of the United Nations, relationship among which shall be based on respect for the principle of sovereign equality.

Article 79

The terms of trusteeship for each territory to be placed under the trusteeship system, including any alteration or amendment, shall be agreed upon by the states directly concerned, including the mandatory power in the case of territories held under mandate by a Member of the United Nations, and shall be approved as provided for in Articles 83 and 85.

Article 80

1. Except as may be agreed upon in individual trusteeship agreements, made under Articles 77, 79, and 81, placing each territory under the trusteeship system, and until such agreements have been concluded, nothing in this Chapter shall be construed in or of itself to alter in any manner the rights whatsoever of any states or any peoples or the terms of existing international instruments to which Members of the United Nations may respectively be parties.

2. Paragraph 1 of this Article shall not be interpreted as giving grounds for delay or postponement of the negotiation and conclusion of agreements for placing mandated and other territories under the trusteeship system as provided for in Article 77.

Article 81

The trusteeship agreement shall in each case include the terms under which the trust territory will be administered and designate the authority which will exercise the administration of the trust territory. Such authority, hereinafter called the administering authority, may be one or more states or the Organization itself.

Article 82

There may be designated, in any trusteeship agreement, a strategic area or areas which may include part or all of the trust territory to which the agreement applies, without prejudice to any special agreement or agreements made under Article 43.

Article 83

1. All functions of the United Nations relating to strategic areas, including the approval of the terms of the trusteeship agreements and of their alteration or amendment, shall be exercised by the Security Council.
2. The basic objectives set forth in Article 76 shall be applicable to the people of each strategic area.
3. The Security Council shall, subject to the provisions of the trusteeship agreements and without prejudice to security considerations, avail itself of the assistance of the Trusteeship Council to perform those functions of the United Nations under the trusteeship system relating to political, economic, social, and educational matters in the strategic areas.

Article 84

It shall be the duty of the administering authority to ensure that the trust territory shall play its part in the maintenance of international peace and security. To this end the administering authority may make use of volunteer forces, facilities, and assistance from the trust territory in carrying out the obligations towards the Security Council undertaken in this regard by the administering authority, as well as for local defense and the maintenance of law and order within the trust territory.

Article 85

1. The functions of the United Nations with regard to trusteeship agreements for all areas not designated as strategic, including the approval of the terms of the trusteeship agreements and of their alteration or amendment, shall be exercised by the General Assembly.
2. The Trusteeship Council, operating under the authority of the General Assembly, shall assist the General Assembly in carrying out these functions.

Chapter XIII
The Trusteeship Council

Composition

Article 86

1. The Trusteeship Council shall consist of the following Members of the United Nations:

a. those Members administering trust territories;

b. such of those Members mentioned by name in Article 23 as are not administering trust territories; and

c. as many other Members elected for three-year terms by the General Assembly as may be necessary to ensure that the total number of members of the Trusteeship Council is equally divided between those Members of the United Nations which administer trust territories and those which do not.

2. Each member of the Trusteeship Council shall designate one specially qualified person to represent it therein.

Functions and Powers

Article 87

The General Assembly and, under its authority, the Trusteeship Council, in carrying out their functions, may:

a. consider reports submitted by the administering authority;

b. accept petitions and examine them in consultation with the administering authority;

c. provide for periodic visits to the respective trust territories at times agreed upon with the administering authority; and

d. take these and other actions in conformity with the terms of the trusteeship agreements.

Article 88

The Trusteeship Council shall formulate a questionnaire on the political, economic, social, and educational advancement of the inhabitants of each trust territory, and the administering authority for each trust territory within the competence of the General Assembly shall make an annual report to the General Assembly upon the basis of such questionnaire.

Voting

Article 89

1. Each member of the Trusteeship Council shall have one vote.
2. Decisions of the Trusteeship Council shall be made by a majority of the members present and voting.

Procedure

Article 90

1. The Trusteeship Council shall adopt its own rules of procedure, including the method of selecting its President.
2. The Trusteeship Council shall meet as required in accordance with its rules, which shall include provision for the convening of meetings on the request of a majority of its members.

Article 91

The Trusteeship Council shall, when appropriate, avail itself of the assistance of the Economic and Social Council and of the specialized agencies in regard to matters with which they are respectively concerned.

Chapter XIV
The International Court of Justice

Article 92

The International Court of Justice shall be the principal judicial organ of the United Nations. It shall function in accordance with the annexed Statute which is based upon the Statute of the Permanent Court of International Justice and forms an integral part of the present Charter.

Article 93

1. All Members of the United Nations are ipso facto parties to the Statute of the International Court of Justice.
2. A state which is not a Member of the United Nations may become a party to the Statute of the International Court of Justice on conditions to be determined in each case by the General Assembly upon the recommendation of the Security Council.

Article 94

1. Each Member of the United Nations undertakes to comply with the decision of the International Court of Justice in any case to which it is a party.
2. If any party to a case fails to perform the obligations incumbent upon it under a judgment rendered by the Court, the other party may have recourse to the Security Council, which may, if it deems necessary, make recommendations or decide upon measures to be taken to give effect to the judgment.

Article 95

Nothing in the present Charter shall prevent Members of the United Nations from entrusting the solution of their differences to other tribunals by virtue of agreements already in existence or which may be concluded in the future.

Article 96

1. The General Assembly or the Security Council may request the International Court of Justice to give an advisory opinion on any legal question.
2. Other organs of the United Nations and specialized agencies, which may at any time be so authorized by the General Assembly, may also request advisory opinions of the Court on legal questions arising within the scope of their activities.

Chapter XV
The Secretariat

Article 97

The Secretariat shall comprise a Secretary-General and such staff as the Organization may require. The Secretary-General shall be appointed by the General Assembly upon the recommendation of the Security Council. He shall be the chief administrative officer of the Organization.

Article 98

The Secretary-General shall act in that capacity in all meetings of the General Assembly, of the Security Council, of the Economic and Social Council, and of the Trusteeship Council, and shall perform such other functions as are entrusted to him by these organs. The Secretary-General shall make an annual report to the General Assembly on the work of the Organization.

Article 99

The Secretary-General may bring to the attention of the Security Council any matter which in his opinion may threaten the maintenance of international peace and security.

Article 100

1. In the performance of their duties the Secretary-General and the staff shall not seek or receive instructions from any government or from any other authority external to the Organization. They shall refrain from any action which might reflect on their position as international officials responsible only to the Organization.
2. Each Member of the United Nations undertakes to respect the exclusively international character of the responsibilities of the Secretary-General and the staff and not to seek to influence them in the discharge of their responsibilities.

Article 101

1. The staff shall be appointed by the Secretary-General under regulations established by the General Assembly.
2. Appropriate staffs shall be permanently assigned to the Economic and Social Council, the Trusteeship Council, and, as required, to other organs of the United Nations. These staffs shall form a part of the Secretariat.
3. The paramount consideration in the employment of the staff and in the determination of the conditions of service shall be the necessity of securing the highest standards of efficiency, competence, and integrity. Due regard shall be paid to the importance of recruiting the staff on as wide a geographical basis as possible.

Chapter XVI
Miscellaneous Provisions

Article 102

1. Every treaty and every international agreement entered into by any Member of the United Nations after the present Charter comes into force shall as soon as possible be registered with the Secretariat and published by it.
2. No party to any such treaty or international agreement which has not been registered in accordance with the provisions of paragraph I of this

Article may invoke that treaty or agreement before any organ of the United Nations.

Article 103

In the event of a conflict between the obligations of the Members of the United Nations under the present Charter and their obligations under any other international agreement, their obligations under the present Charter shall prevail.

Article 104

The Organization shall enjoy in the territory of each of its Members such legal capacity as may be necessary for the exercise of its functions and the fulfillment of its purposes.

Article 105

1. The Organization shall enjoy in the territory of each of its Members such privileges and immunities as are necessary for the fulfillment of its purposes.
2. Representatives of the Members of the United Nations and officials of the Organization shall similarly enjoy such privileges and immunities as are necessary for the independent exercise of their functions in connection with the Organization.
3. The General Assembly may make recommendations with a view to determining the details of the application of paragraphs 1 and 2 of this Article or may propose conventions to the Members of the United Nations for this purpose.

Chapter XVII
Transitional Security Arrangements
Article 106

Pending the coming into force of such special agreements referred to in Article 43 as in the opinion of the Security Council enable it to begin the exercise of its responsibilities under Article 42, the parties to the Four-Nation Declaration, signed at Moscow October 30, 1943, and France, shall, in accordance with the provisions of paragraph 5 of that Declaration, consult with one another and as occasion requires with other Members of the United Nations with a view to such joint action on behalf of the Organization as may be necessary for the purpose of maintaining international peace and security.

Article 107

Nothing in the present Charter shall invalidate or preclude action, in relation to any state which during the Second World War has been an enemy of any signatory to the present Charter, taken or authorized as a result of that war by the Governments having responsibility for such action.

Chapter XVIII
Amendments

Article 108

Amendments to the present Charter shall come into force for all Members of the United Nations when they have been adopted by a vote of two-thirds of the members of the General Assembly and ratified in accordance with their respective constitutional processes by two-thirds of the Members of the United Nations, including all the permanent members of the Security Council.

Article 109

1. A General Conference of the Members of the United Nations for the purpose of reviewing the present Charter may be held at a date and place to be fixed by a two-thirds vote of the members of the General Assembly and by a vote of any seven members of the Security Council. Each Member of the United Nations shall have one vote in the conference.

2. Any alteration of the present Charter recommended by a two-thirds vote of the conference shall take effect when ratified in accordance with their respective constitutional processes by two-thirds of the Members of the United Nations including all the permanent members of the Security Council.

3. If such a conference has not been held before the tenth annual session of the General Assembly following the coming into force of the present Charter, the proposal to call such a conference shall be placed on the agenda of that session of the General Assembly, and the conference shall be held if so decided by a majority vote of the members of the General Assembly and by a vote of any seven members of the Security Council.

Chapter XIX
Ratification and Signature

Article 110

1. The present Charter shall be ratified by the signatory states in accordance with their respective constitutional processes.

2. The ratifications shall be deposited with the Government of the United States of America, which shall notify all the signatory states of each deposit as well as the Secretary-General of the Organization when he has been appointed.

3. The present Charter shall come into force upon the deposit of ratifications by the Republic of China, France, the Union of Soviet Socialist Republics, the United Kingdom of Great Britain and Northern Ireland, and the United States of America, and by a majority of the other signatory states. A protocol of the ratifications deposited shall thereupon be drawn up by the Government of the United States of America which shall communicate copies thereof to all the signatory states.

4. The states signatory to the present Charter which ratify it after it has come into force will become original Members of the United Nations on the date of the deposit of their respective ratifications.

Article 111

The present Charter, of which the Chinese, French, Russian, English, and Spanish texts are equally authentic, shall remain deposited in the archives of the Government of the United States of America. Duly certified copies thereof shall be transmitted by that Government to the Governments of the other signatory states.

IN FAITH WHEREOF the representatives of the Governments of the United Nations have signed the present Charter.

DONE at the city of San Francisco the twenty-sixth day of June, one thousand nine hundred and forty-five.

Further Reading

INTRODUCTION

Customary international law
Michael Akehurst, 'Custom as a Source of International Law', (1974–75), 47, *British Yearbook of International Law*, 1
Michael Byers, *Custom, Power and the Power of Rules: International Relations and Customary International Law* (Cambridge University Press, 1999)
Gennady Danilenko, *Law-Making in the International Community* (Martinus Nijhoff, 1993)

Law of treaties
Lord McNair, *The Law of Treaties* (Oxford University Press, 1961, reprinted 1986)
1969 Vienna Convention on the Law of Treaties, 1155 United Nations Treaty Series, also available at:
<http://www.un.org/law/ilc/texts/treatfra.htm>
Paul Reuter, *Introduction to the Law of Treaties* (2nd English edn), trans. José Mico and Peter Haggenmacher (Kegan Paul International, 1995)
Oscar Schachter, 'Entangled Treaty and Custom', in *International Law at a Time of Perplexity: Essays in Honour of Shabtai Rosenne,* ed. Yoram Dinstein (Martinus Nijhoff, Dordrecht, 1989), p. 717

International law on the use of force
Ian Brownlie, *International Law and the Use of Force by States* (Oxford University Press, 1963)
Yoram Dinstein, *War, Aggression and Self-Defence* (3rd edn, Cambridge University Press, 2001)
Thomas M. Franck, *Recourse to Force* (Cambridge University Press, 2003)
Christine Gray, *International Law and the Use of Force* (2nd edn, Oxford University Press, 2004)

International humanitarian law
Yoram Dinstein, *The Conduct of Hostilities under the Law of International Armed Conflict* (Cambridge University Press, 2004)
A. P. V. Rogers, *Law on the Battlefield* (2nd edn) (Manchester University Press, 2004)

War law and the United States
Michael Byers and Georg Nolte (eds), *United States Hegemony and the Foundations of International Law* (Cambridge University Press, 2003)

1: SECURITY COUNCIL AUTHORIZATION

United Nations and the use of force
Danesh Sarooshi, *The United Nations and the Development of Collective Security: The Delegation by the UN Security Council of its Chapter VII Powers* (Oxford University Press, 1999)
Bruno Simma (ed.), *The Charter of the United Nations: A Commentary* (2nd edn, Oxford University Press, 2002)

Korea
Country profile: North Korea <http://news.bbc.co.uk/1/hi/world/asia-pacific/country_profiles/1131421.stm>
Timeline: North Korea <http://news.bbc.co.uk/1/hi/world/asia-pacific/country_profiles/1132268.stm>
Country profile: South Korea <http://news.bbc.co.uk/1/hi/world/asia-pacific/country_profiles/1123668.stm>
Timeline: South Korea <http://news.bbc.co.uk/1/hi/world/asia-pacific/country_profiles/1132724.stm>
Edwin C. Hoyt, 'The United States Reaction to the Korean Attack: A Study of the Principles of the United Nations Charter as a Factor in American Policy-Making' (1961), 55, *American Journal of International Law*, 45

Southern Rhodesia
Country profile: Zimbabwe <http://news.bbc.co.uk/2/hi/world/africa/country_profiles/1064589.stm>
Timeline: Zimbabwe <http://news.bbc.co.uk/2/hi/world/africa/country_profiles/1831470.stm>

Vera Gowlland-Debbas, *Collective Responses to Illegal Acts in International Law: United Nations Action in the Question of Southern Rhodesia* (Martinus Nijhoff, 1990)

Myres McDougal and W. Michael Reisman, 'Rhodesia and the United Nations: The Lawfulness of International Concern' (1968), 62, *American Journal of International Law*, 1

Iraq (1990–91)

Country profile: Iraq <http://news.bbc.co.uk/1/hi/world/middle-east/country_profiles/791014.stm>

Timeline: Iraq <http://news.bbc.co.uk/1/hi/world/middle-east/country_profiles/737483.stm>

Oscar Schachter, 'United Nations Law in the Gulf Conflict' (1991), 85, *American Journal of International Law*, 452

Marc Weller (ed.), *Iraq and Kuwait: The Hostilities and their Aftermath* (Grotius, 1993)

Bosnia-Herzegovina

Country profile: Bosnia-Herzegovina <http://news.bbc.co.uk/1/hi/world/europe/country_profiles/1066886.stm>

Timeline: Bosnia-Herzegovina <http://news.bbc.co.uk/1/hi/world/europe/country_profiles/1066981.stm>

Simon Chesterman, *Just War or Just Peace? Humanitarian Intervention and International Law* (Oxford University Press, 2001)

2: EXPANDING REACH OF THE SECURITY COUNCIL

Somalia

Country profile: Somalia <http://news.bbc.co.uk/1/hi/world/africa/country_profiles/1072592.stm>

Timeline: Somalia <http://news.bbc.co.uk/1/hi/world/africa/country_profiles/1072611.stm>

Ruth Gordon, 'United Nations Intervention in Internal Conflicts: Iraq, Somalia, and Beyond' (1994), 15, *Michigan Journal of International Law*, 519

Rwanda

Country profile: Rwanda <http://news.bbc.co.uk/1/hi/world/africa/country_profiles/1070265.stm>

Timeline: Rwanda <http://news.bbc.co.uk/1/hi/world/africa/country_profiles/1070329.stm>

Roméo Dallaire, *Shake Hands with the Devil: The Failure of Humanity in Rwanda* (Random House, 2003)

Linda Melvern, *A People Betrayed: The Role of the West in Rwanda's Genocide* (Zed Books, 2000)

Haiti

Country profile: Haiti <http://news.bbc.co.uk/2/hi/world/americas/country_profiles/1202772.stm>

Timeline: Haiti <http://news.bbc.co.uk/2/hi/americas/1202857.stm>

Gregory H. Fox and Brad R. Roth (eds), *Democratic Governance and International Law* (Cambridge University Press, 2000)

David Malone, *Decision-Making in the UN Security Council: The Case of Haiti, 1990–1997* (Oxford University Press, 1998)

W. Michael Reisman, 'Haiti and the Validity of International Action' (1995), 89, *American Journal of International Law*, 82

East Timor

Country profile: East Timor <http://news.bbc.co.uk/1/hi/world/asia-pacific/country_profiles/1508119.stm>

Timeline: East Timor <http://news.bbc.co.uk/1/hi/world/asia-pacific/country_profiles/1508119.stm>

Mark Rothert, 'U.N. Intervention in East Timor' (2000), 39, *Columbia Journal of Transnational Law*, 257

Darfur, Sudan

Human Rights Watch, 'Empty Promises: Continuing Abuses in Darfur, Sudan', HRW Briefing Paper, 11 August 2004 <http://hrw.org/backgrounder/africa/sudan/2004/>

International Crisis Group, 'Darfur Deadline: A New International Action Plan', ICG Africa Report No. 83, 23 August 2004 <http://www.crisisweb.org/home/index.cfm>

Samantha Power, 'Dying in Darfur', *New Yorker*, 30 August 2004, pp. 56–73

3: Implied Authorization and Intentional Ambiguity

No-fly zones in Iraq
Christine Gray, 'After the Ceasefire: Iraq, the Security Council and the Use of Force' (1994), 65, *British Yearbook of International Law*, 135
Jules Lobel and Michael Ratner, 'Bypassing the Security Council: Ambiguous Authorization to Use Force, Cease-Fires and the Iraqi Inspection Regime' (1999), 93, *American Journal of International Law*, 124

Kosovo (1999)
BBC News, 'Kosovo: An Uneasy Peace' <http://news.bbc.co.uk/hi/english/static/kosovo_fact_files/default.stm>
Simon Chesterman, *Just War or Just Peace? Humanitarian Intervention and International Law* (Oxford University Press, 2001)
Dino Kritsiotis, 'The Kosovo Crisis and NATO's application of armed force against the Federal Republic of Yugoslavia' (2000), 49, *International and Comparative Law Quarterly*, 330

Iraq (2003)
BBC News, 'Iraq in Transition' <http://news.bbc.co.uk/1/hi/in_depth/middle_east/2002/conflict_with_iraq/default.stm>
Dino Kritsiotis, 'Arguments of Mass Confusion' (2004), 15, *European Journal of International Law*, 233
Jane Stromseth, 'Law and Force After Iraq: A Transitional Moment' (2003), 97, *American Journal of International Law*, 628

Interpretation of Security Council resolutions
Jochen Abr. Frowein, 'Unilateral Interpretation of Security Council Resolutions – A Threat to Collective Security?' in Volkmar Götz (ed.), *Liber amicorum Günther Jaenicke – zum 85. Geburtstag* (Springer, 1998) p. 98
Michael Wood, 'The Interpretation of Security Council Resolutions' (1998), 2, *Max Planck United Nations Yearbook*, 73

4: 'Inherent Right' of Self-defence

The Caroline *incident*
R. Y. Jennings, 'The *Caroline* and McLeod Cases' (1938), 32, *American Journal of International Law*, 82

Protection of nationals

Michael Akehurst, 'The use of force to protect nationals abroad' (1977), 5, *International Relations*, 3

Derek Bowett, 'The Use of Force for the Protection of Nationals Abroad' in Antonio Cassese (ed.), *The Current Legal Regulation of the Use of Force* (Martinus Nijhoff, 1986), p. 39

Self-defence and reprisals

R. Barsotti, 'Armed Reprisals' in Antonio Cassese (ed.), *The Current Legal Regulation of the Use of Force* (Martinus Nijhoff, 1986), p. 79

Dino Kritsiotis, 'The Legality of the 1993 Missile Strike on Iraq and the Right of Self-Defence in International Law' (1996), 45, *International and Comparative Law Quarterly*, p. 163

5: SELF-DEFENCE AGAINST TERRORISM

Libya (1986)

Country profile: Libya <http://news.bbc.co.uk/1/hi/world/middle_east/country_profiles/819291.stm>

Timeline: Libya <http://news.bbc.co.uk/1/hi/world/middle_east/country_profiles/1398437.stm>

Abraham Sofaer, 'Terrorism and the Law' (1986), *Foreign Affairs*, 901

David Turndorf, 'The U.S. Raid on Libya: A Forceful Response' (1988), 14, *Brooklyn Journal of International Law*, 187

Afghanistan and Sudan (1998)

Country profile: Afghanistan <http://news.bbc.co.uk/1/hi/world/south_asia/country_profiles/1162668.stm>

Timeline: Afghanistan <http://news.bbc.co.uk/1/hi/world/south_asia/1162108.stm>

Country profile: Sudan <http://news.bbc.co.uk/1/hi/world/middle_east/country_profiles/820864.stm>

Timeline: Sudan <http://news.bbc.co.uk/1/hi/world/middle_east/country_profiles/827425.stm>

Jules Lobel, 'The Use of Force to Respond to Terrorist Attacks: The Bombing of Sudan and Afghanistan' (1999), 24, *Yale Journal of International Law*, 537

Ruth Wedgwood, 'Responding to Terrorism: The Strikes Against bin Laden' (1999), 24, *Yale Journal of International Law*, 559

Afghanistan (2001)

Michael Byers, 'Terrorism, the Use of Force and International Law after 11 September' (2002), 51, *International and Comparative Law Quarterly*, 401; reprinted in (2002) 16, *International Relations*, 155

Thomas Franck, 'Terrorism and the Right of Self-Defense' (2001), 95, *American Journal of International Law*, 839

Israel, Palestine and 'targeted killings'

Country profile: Israel and Palestinian Territories <http://news.bbc.co.uk/1/hi/world/middle_east/country_profiles/803257.stm>

Amnesty International, *Israel and the Occupied Territories: State Assassinations and Other Unlawful Killings* (AI Index No. MDE 15/005/2001, February 2001) <http://web.amnesty.org/library/index/engmde150052001>

Eyal Benvenisti, *The International Law of Occupation* (Princeton University Press, 1993; reprinted in 2004 with a new preface)

Adam Roberts, 'Prolonged Military Occupation: The Israeli-Occupied Territories Since 1967' (1990), 84, *American Journal of International Law*, 44

Michael Schmitt, 'State-Sponsored Assassination in International and Domestic Law' (1992), 17, *Yale Journal of International Law*, 609

6: PRE-EMPTIVE SELF-DEFENCE

The Caroline *Case and Article 51*

Derek Bowett, *Self-defence in International Law* (Manchester University Press, 1958)

Ian Brownlie, *International Law and the Use of Force by States* (Oxford University Press, 1963)

Osirak nuclear reactor (1981)

Timothy MacCormack, *Self-defense in international law: the Israeli raid on the Iraqi nuclear reactor* (St. Martin's Press, New York, 1986)

Bush Doctrine and National Security Strategy of the United States (2002)

Christopher Greenwood, 'International Law and Preemptive Use of Force: Afghanistan, Al-Qaida and Iraq' (2003), 4, *San Diego International Law Journal*, 7

National Security Strategy of the United States, September 2002 <http://www.whitehouse.gov/nsc/nss.pdf>

Report of the Secretary General's High Level Panel on Threats, Challenges and Change, *A more secure world: Our shared responsibility* (United Nations, 2004) <http://www.un.org/secureworld>

Ruth Wedgwood, 'The Fall of Saddam Hussein: Security Council Mandates and Preemptive Self-Defence' (2003), 97, *American Journal of International Law*, 576

7: PRO-DEMOCRATIC INTERVENTION

Pro-democratic intervention in general

James Crawford, 'Democracy and International Law' (1993), 44, *British Yearbook of International Law*, 113

Gregory Fox and Brad Roth (eds), *Democratic Governance and International Law* (Cambridge University Press, 2000)

Thomas Franck, *Fairness in International Law and Institutions* (Oxford University Press, 1995)

Brad Roth, *Government Illegitimacy in International Law* (Oxford University Press, 1999)

Oscar Schachter, 'The Legality of Pro-Democratic Invasion' (1984), 78, *American Journal of International Law*, 645

Grenada

Country profile: Grenada <http://news.bbc.co.uk/2/hi/americas/country_profiles/1209605.stm>

Timeline: Grenada <http://news.bbc.co.uk/2/hi/americas/country_profiles/1209649.stm>

Robert Beck, 'International Law and the Decision to Invade Grenada: A Ten-Year Retrospective' (1993), 33, *Virginia Journal of International Law*, 789

'Legal Adviser of the Department of State, Davis R. Robinson, letter dated February 10, 1984, addressed to Professor Edward Gordon, Chairman of the Committee on Grenada of the American Bar Association's Section on International Law and Practice' (1984), 78, *American Journal of International Law*, 661

Panama

Country profile: Panama <http://news.bbc.co.uk/2/hi/world/americas/country_profiles/1229332.stm>

Timeline: Panama <http://news.bbc.co.uk/2/hi/world/americas/1229333.stm>

Anthony D'Amato, 'The Invasion of Panama Was a Lawful Response to Tyranny' (1990), 84, *American Journal of International Law*, 516

Louis Henkin, 'The Invasion of Panama under International Law: A Gross Violation' (1991), 29, *Columbia Journal of Transnational Law*, 293

W. Michael Reisman, 'Sovereignty and Human Rights in Contemporary International Law' (1990), 84, *American Journal of International Law*, 866

8: UNILATERAL HUMANITARIAN INTERVENTION

Humanitarian intervention in general

Simon Chesterman, *Just War or Just Peace? Humanitarian Intervention and International Law* (Oxford University Press, 2001)

J. L. Holzgrefe and Robert O. Keohane, *Humanitarian Intervention: Ethical, Legal, and Political Dilemmas* (Cambridge University Press, 2003)

Sean Murphy, *Humanitarian Intervention: The United Nations in an Evolving World Order* (University of Pennsylvania Press, 1996)

Adam Roberts, 'The So-called "Right" of Humanitarian Intervention' (2000), 3, *Yearbook of International Humanitarian Law*, 3

Nicholas Wheeler, *Saving Strangers: Humanitarian Intervention in International Society* (Oxford University Press, 2000)

East Pakistan (1971)

Country profile: Bangladesh <http://news.bbc.co.uk/1/hi/world/south_asia/country_profiles/1160598.stm>

Timeline: Bangladesh <http://news.bbc.co.uk/1/hi/world/south_asia/country_profiles/1160896.stm>

Thomas Franck and Nigel Rodley, 'After Bangladesh: The Law of Humanitarian Intervention by Military Force' (1973), 67, *American Journal of International Law*, 275

Cambodia (1978)
Country profile: Cambodia <http://news.bbc.co.uk/1/hi/world/asia-pacific/country_profiles/1243892.stm>
Timeline: Cambodia <http://news.bbc.co.uk/1/hi/world/asia-pacific/country_profiles/1244006.stm>
Gary Klintworth, *Vietnam's Intervention in Cambodia in International Law* (Australian Government Publishing Service, 1989)

Uganda (1979)
Country profile: Uganda <http://news.bbc.co.uk/1/hi/world/africa/country_profiles/1069166.stm>
Timeline: Uganda <http://news.bbc.co.uk/1/hi/world/africa/country_profiles/1069181.stm>
U. O. Umozurike, 'Tanzania's Intervention in Uganda' (1982), 20, *Archiv des Völkerrecht*, 301

Kosovo (1999)
Kosovo: An Uneasy Peace <http://news.bbc.co.uk/hi/english/static/kosovo_fact_files/default.stm>
The Kosovo Report: Report of the Independent International Commission on Kosovo (Oxford University Press, 2000)

9: RESPONSIBILITY TO PROTECT

The Responsibility to Protect: Report of the International Commission on Intervention and State Sovereignty (Ottawa: International Development Research Centre, 2001)
The Kosovo Report: Report of the Independent International Commission on Kosovo (Oxford University Press, 2000)
Report of the Secretary General's High Level Panel on Threats, Challenges and Change, *A more secure world: Our shared responsibility* (United Nations, 2004) <http://www.un.org/secureworld>
Lloyd Axworthy, *Navigating a New World: Canada's Global Future* (Alfred A. Knopf, Canada, 2003)
Terry Nardin, 'The Moral Basis of Humanitarian Intervention' (2002), 16, *Ethics and International Affairs*, 57
W. Michael Reisman, 'Sovereignty and Human Rights in Contemporary International Law' (1990), 84, *American Journal of International Law*, 866

Fernando Tesón, *Humanitarian Intervention: An Inquiry into Law and Morality* (2nd edn, Transnational Publishers, 1997)

Nicholas Wheeler, *Saving Strangers: Humanitarian Intervention in International Society* (Oxford University Press, 2000)

10: PROTECTION OF CIVILIANS

Geoffrey Best, *War and Law since 1945* (Oxford University Press, 1997)

Crimes of War Project <http://www.crimesofwar.org/>

Yoram Dinstein, *The Conduct of Hostilities under the Law of International Armed Conflict* (Cambridge University Press, 2004)

Roy Gutman and David Rieff, *Crimes of War: What the Public Should Know* (W. W. Norton & Co., 1999)

International Committee of the Red Cross: <http://www.icrc.org/>

A. P. V. Rogers, *Law on the Battlefield* (2nd edn, Manchester University Press, 2004)

Marco Sassoli and Antoine Bouvier, *How Does Law Protect in War?* (International Committee of the Red Cross, 1999)

UK Ministry of Defence, *The Manual of the Law of Armed Conflict* (Oxford University Press, 2004)

11: PROTECTION OF COMBATANTS AND PRISONERS OF WAR

Geoffrey Best, *War and Law since 1945* (Oxford University Press, 1997)

Crimes of War Project <http://www.crimesofwar.org/>

Yoram Dinstein, *The Conduct of Hostilities under the Law of International Armed Conflict* (Cambridge University Press, 2004)

Roy Gutman and David Rieff, *Crimes of War: What the Public Should Know* (W. W. Norton & Co., 1999)

Seymour Hersh, *Chain of Command: The Road from 9/11 to Abu Ghraib* (HarperCollins, 2004)

International Committee of the Red Cross <http://www.icrc.org/>

A. P. V. Rogers, *Law on the Battlefield* (2nd edn, Manchester University Press, 2004)

Marco Sassoli and Antoine Bouvier, *How Does Law Protect in War?* (International Committee of the Red Cross, 1999)

UK Ministry of Defence, *The Manual of the Law of Armed Conflict* (Oxford University Press, 2004)

12: War Crimes Courts and Tribunals

Bruce Broomhall, *International Justice and the International Criminal Court: Between Sovereignty and the Rule of Law* (Oxford University Press, 2003)

Antonio Cassese, Paola Gaeta and John Jones, *The Rome Statute of the International Criminal Court: A Commentary* (Oxford University Press, 2002)

Steven R. Ratner and Jason S. Abrams, *Accountability for Human Rights Atrocities in International Law* (2nd edn, Oxford University Press, 2001)

Geoffrey Robertson QC, *Crimes Against Humanity: The Struggle for Global Justice* (2nd edn, Penguin, 2002)

William Schabas, *An Introduction to the International Criminal Court* (Cambridge University Press, 2001)

Chris Stephen, *Judgement Day: The Trial of Slobodan Milošević* (Atlantic Books, 2004)

Epilogue: War Law and the Single Superpower

Michael Byers and Georg Nolte (eds), *United States Hegemony and the Foundations of International Law* (Cambridge University Press, 2003)

Wilhelm G. Grewe, *The Epochs of International Law*, translated & revised by Michael Byers (Walter De Gruyter, 2000)

Christian Reus-Smit, *American Power and World Order* (Polity Press, 2004)

Selected Internet Sites

Academic Council of the United Nations System
<http://www.acuns.wlu.ca>

American Society of International Law <http://www.asil.org>

Amnesty International <http://amnesty.org>

British Institute of International and Comparative Law
<http://www.biicl.org>

Carnegie Council on Ethics and International Affairs
<http://www.carnegiecouncil.org>

Carnegie Endowment for International Peace <http://www.ceip.org/>

Chatham House <http://www.chathamhouse.org.uk>

Council on Foreign Relations <http://www.cfr.org/>

Crimes of War Project <http://www.crimesofwar.org>

Foreign and Commonwealth Office, London <http://www.fco.gov.uk>

Human Rights Watch <http://www.hrw.org>

International Committee of the Red Cross <http://www.icrc.org>

ICRC databases on international humanitarian law
<http://www.icrc.org/web/eng/siteengo.nsf/iwplList2/
Info_recources:IHL_databases>

1949 Geneva Conventions and 1977 Protocols
<http://www.icrc.org/Web/Eng/siteeng0.nsf/html/genevaconventions>

International Court of Justice <http://www.icj-cij.org>

International Criminal Court <http://www.icc-cpi.int>

International Criminal Tribunal for the Former Yugoslavia
<http://www.un.org/icty>

International Criminal Tribunal for Rwanda <http://www.ictr.org>

International Humanitarian Law Research Initiative
<http://www.ihlresearch.org/ihl>

International Institute for Strategic Studies <http://www.iiss.org>

International Law Association <http://www.ila-hq.org>

International Peace Academy <http://www.ipacademy.org/>

Iraqi Special Tribunal Statute
<http://www.cpa-iraq.org/human_rights/Statute.htm>

Lauterpacht Research Centre for International Law, Cambridge
<http://www.law.cam.ac.uk/rcil>

Max Planck Institute for Comparative Public Law and International Law
<http://www.virtual-institute.de/eindex.cfm>

North Atlantic Treaty Organization <http://www.nato.int/>

Special Court for Sierra Leone <http://www.sc-sl.org>

Stockholm International Peace Research Institute <http://www.sipri.se>

T. M. C. Asser Institute (The Hague) <http://www.asser.nl>

United Nations:

UN General Assembly <http://www.un.org/ga>

UN Security Council <http://www.un.org/Docs/sc>

UN Security Council Resolutions
<http://www.un.org/documents/scres.htm>

UN Secretary General
<http://www.un.org/News/ossg/sg/index.shtml>

United Nations Association of the United States of America:
<http://www.unausa.org>

United States Department of Defense <http://www.dod.gov>

United States Department of State <http://www.state.gov>

Index

RENNER LEARNING RESOURCE CENTER
ELGIN COMMUNITY COLLEGE
ELGIN, ILLINOIS 60123

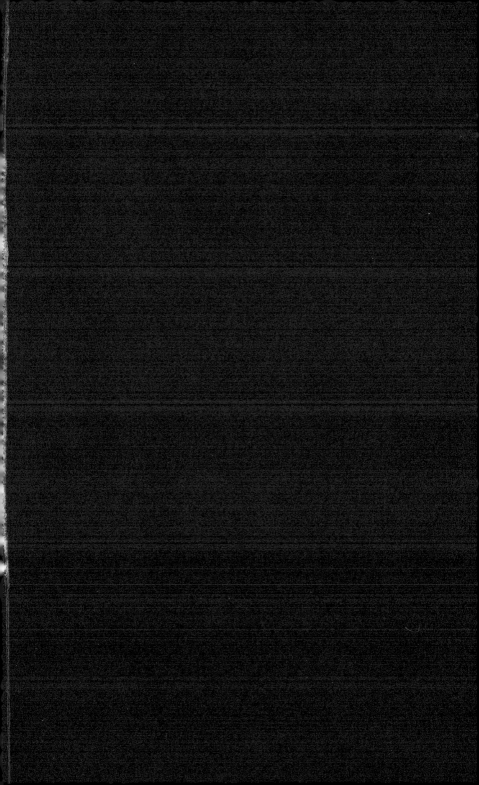